Reassembling Still

OTHER WORKS BY DAVID MILLER INCLUDE

The Caryatids: Poems 1971-73, Enitharmon Press, London, 1975
All My Life, Joe di Maggio Press, London, 1975
Our Bread, Actual Size Press, Deal, Kent, 1976
Malcolm Lowry and the Voyage that Never Ends, Enitharmon Press, 1976
Out of this World: Eight Prose Texts, 1977-1980, Spectacular Diseases Press, Peterborough, 1984
W. H. Hudson and the Elusive Paradise, Macmillan, London / St. Martin's Press, New York, NY, 1990
Cards (with John Levy), Sow's Ear, Stafford, 1991
True Points: Eight Prose Texts 1981-1987, Spectacular Diseases Press, 1992
Tesserae, Stride Publications, Exeter, 1993
Art and Disclosure: Seven Essays, Stride, 1998
Commentaries, tel-let, Charleston, IL, 1999
Commentaries (II), Runaway Spoon Press, Port Charlotte, FL, 2000
The Waters of Marah: Selected Prose 1973-1995, Shearsman Books, Exeter, 2005
The Dorothy and Benno Stories, Reality Street Editions, Hastings, 2005
British Poetry Magazines 1914-2000: A History and Bibliography of 'Little Magazines' (with Richard Price), The British Library, London / Oak Knoll Press, New Castle, DE, 2006
Spiritual Letters (Series 1-5), Chax Press, Tucson, AZ, 2011
Black, Grey and White: A Book of Visual Sonnets, Veer Books, London, 2011
Spiritual Letters (Series 1-5) (Audio Recording, Double CD), LARYNX, London, 2012
GLORIA and other early poems, erbacce-press, Liverpool, 2013
A River Flowing Beside, hawkhaven press, San Francisco, CA, 2014

EDITED BY DAVID MILLER

A Curious Architecture: a selection of contemporary prose poems (with Rupert Loydell), Stride, 1996
The ABCs of Robert Lax (with Nicholas Zurbrugg), Stride, 1999
Music while drowning: German Expressionist Poems (with Stephen Watts), Tate Publishing, London, 2003
The Lariat and other writings by Jaime de Angulo, Counterpoint, Berkeley, CA, 2009
The Alchemist's Mind: a book of narrative prose by poets, Reality Street, 2012

DAVID MILLER

Reassembling Still
Collected Poems

For Gloria

*all good wishes,
David.*

Shearsman Books

First published in the United Kingdom in 2014 by
Shearsman Books Ltd
50 Westons Hill Drive
Emersons Green
BRISTOL
BS16 7DF

Shearsman Books Ltd Registered Office
30–31 St. James Place, Mangotsfield, Bristol BS16 9JB
(this address not for correspondence)

www.shearsman.com

ISBN 978-1-84861-331-7

Copyright © David Miller, 1974, 1975, 1976, 1977, 1979, 1980, 1981,1982, 1984, 1985, 1986, 1988, 1989, 1991, 1992, 1993, 1994, 1995, 1996, 1997, 2000, 2003, 2004, 2006, 2007, 2009, 2013, 2014.

The right of David Miller to be identified as the author of this work has been asserted by him in accordance with the Copyrights, Designs and Patents Act of 1988.
All rights reserved.

Cover image, 'Untitled (Blue and Black)' by the author, copyright © 2005, 2014 by David Miller.

Contents

A path a lake the very breath	11
Confrontation	13
Landscape	16
In the Field	17
Fire Water	19
Thesis	22
Suite	25
The London/Hartgrove Notebook	27
(Untitled / for Bill Cirocco)	32
"the drift…"	33
"moving to the margins…"	34
Derivation	35
"long-sustained gazing her eyes…"	36
"he spoke of prophecy's end…"	37
"we stopped at the sea…"	38
"Power…"	39
Wild Poignancy	40
"memory water flowing…"	43
RELATION	45
"3/ swings…"	47
"snow field…"	48
"water to blood…"	49
Hagoromo	50
Elegy	51
The Book of the Spoonmaker	53
Stromata	56
Moments	63
Messages	64
(From:) The Preparation	66
The Story	70
The Music	78

Primavera	82
Insistence	85
Voice	88
Children	91
Moments	94
Pictures of Mercy	97
Participation	100
Plenum	101
Participation	103
Understanding	105
"suddenly…"	108
"and I stopped, how long…"	109
1969	110
What Determines What We Are	111
GLORIA	113
"white surface…"	113
"3 children…"	115
"Chris, his daughter Sarah and I…"	116
"white terrace house opposite…"	117
"flame at one window (fire in the room)…"	118
"February 21 1977, Mathias sent me a postcard…"	119
"solar radiation, wind, rain, gravity…"	120
"reflection…"	121
"cold…"	123
"Apropos of the symbolism…"	124
Areas	126
A Song, for Plumage	138
"the eye sees…"	145
"Someone comes, out of the distance…"	148
"The blinding moment…"	150
Three Poems for Julius Bissier	151
Portals	153
Cells	157
Aura	159
Threshold	162

The Image	164
Bagatelles	165
Appearance & Event: 16 Poems	167
"the length is as large as the breadth…"	168
"Penetration: one…"	169
"The invisible form…"	170
"…external kisses have been made…"	171
"Burning the house down…"	172
"I have polished brass door handles & door-plates…"	173
"Silver lines etched into the night bind us…"	174
"In the night all the given names cut through…"	175
"for George Alexander…"	176
"The narrative is broken by…"	177
"There is a confusion of voices & the voices…"	178
"If the images of friends have returned…"	179
"*She turns everything into wine*, the man said…"	180
"Held by the image I am caught…"	181
"An ambulance…"	182
Poem for Emmy Hennings	183
The Soprano	184
Funeral Music (for R. C. Kenedy)	185
Kiss Me	186
The Oak Tree in the Garden	187
Of the World. Of Power	189
"a mist & a circle of light…"	192
Slides	194
Unity	199
Orientation	201
Background Music	204
Three-Way	210
Audrie Browne	212
A Sort of Beguine	216
Through Fire	218
There and Here	221

"The black oval surface framed in gilt…"	224
"The stones at junctions…"	225
"Set up on a hill: a structure…"	226
"Lights, openings…"	227
"Only through…"	228
"Burnished verticals…"	229
Poem (for Paolo Uccello)	230
Rain	231
"A dust-storm obliterated…"	232
Poem/ (for Faith)	233
" 'Above the earth', she said…"	234
Ballad	235
"He collapsed, lay helpless…"	237
"The window frames…"	238
The Room	239
"On the mountain…"	240
"*Predestination* – a painter gave me…"	241
"In the blue…"	242
"The surviving light…"	243
The Field	244
"Frescobaldi on the organ…"	245
"She came down a stairway, dark…"	246
for J. R. – i. m.	247
"perception (blue…"	248
2 about Music	249
"so then turns away…"	250
"the taste of curds…"	251
"Japanese *raku* bowl…"	252
"what would it mean…"	253
Door of Paradise	254
Legend	256
At the Heart of the Thicket	258
Dark Ground	261
For Patty Waters	265
Devotion	267
Focus	270
Faces	273
The Park	275

South London Mix	276
The Flamingos	293
The Same Again	294
The Cups	295
"Half-turned away through our half-…"	296
Lacunae	297
Vermeer	298
"The burning wood says…"	299
"Beech furnishes the…"	300
"An afternoon with a circus…"	301
"The hour grew more…"	302
"Sunlight dapples the floor…"	303
"To offer: to receive: to eat…"	304
Acknowledgements	306
Notes	308

To the memory of Petros Bourgos

A path a lake the very breath

night fastens upon a window
twice a small path a room
you appear at the gate you follow

down the hallway where
the television's been left
on the top of the closet

amplifications *left and right*
gate-posts two slabs of stone
time deranged and revered

.

chill air deep blue
of conjoined sky
and lake aciculate

a writing of true
derivations the lines
are bestowed as praise

for the lovely (slender)
and good girl
who is my friend

.

the victim suffers
through an image
into desire or injury
and death – your face

your very breath
visible in the cold
commands me abjure
spells dissolve harm

in the *shop of nothing*
by the way of nothing

Confrontation

1.

They have been sitting together for a long while, talking; one of the two drinking wine without offering any and without being asked for it.

– Do you wait as the children in the fable, their parents away and a tiger prowling at the gate? They must sacrifice their livestock to the tiger as others – in the same spirit – propitiate demons, waiting for release from their ordeal.

2.

from the bus she was there
on the balcony at eye-level
but not looking at him

moss and wild strawberry
wild-rose running in a cleft
of Derbyshire limestone

the rose of Demeter
in he remembered
the cleft of her rocks

3.

– you desire to eat
the beautiful as it's
incarnate in flesh

or image – *dignity*
you say and *freedom*
lurid absurd flashes

rebelling against darkness
language caught in the
toils of your violence

4.

the path deviates to a lake
cleared he follows it he's
drawn as by the need

to give testimony he'll
write it down as it falls
as by chance her speech

falling waking in a past
impossible her young
voice its clarity

5.

– your desires coagulate
around death their residence?
with decay and stone signs

turn and see a fresco a devil
shitting into a witch's mouth
but the witch Rangda appears

the face is exposed menaced
and the Barong can only
fight Rangda to no outcome

6.

the wind lifts a line
of small red panels strung
down the building's side

when the night comes
the rain at night drink wine
fall asleep wake and write

and paint in broken ink
the door open and wax
dripping on the table

Landscape

(for Linda Bryant)

a black so chill
it numbs the eye

you favoured rocks
I spoke up
for the comfort of trees

.

in a desert landscape
these Polish lamentations
are lifted breaking
through a wash of static

cholla and prickly-pear
seen from a moving car
the soprano's voice
that sings of grief entire

a confluence unstable
that ear shapes with eye

In the Field

1.

"don't turn away where are you gazing
and whatever are you gazing at?"
"there was a huge golden man"
the girl said "lying down on a couch
and the couch was in a field"

2.

details reproduced through layers levels
the dream coming home in day's hours

3.

a line in vermilion
brushed onto paper
gold body-colour
anticipations of black
on white revealing birds
and immortal beings

4.

"throughout that field there were outbursts
of crying" but the children take on the aspect
of celestial nymphs and a love
from before birth's remembered
unearthly life stirring in faces

5.

and the tribute which he offered
was a picture of the Lord of Heaven
and of the Mother of the Lord
altogether improper things he brought bones
of supernatural beings they are superfluous things
which ought not to enter the palace

6.

disseisin *where were we now*
where else could we be
than in that same field

Fire Water

(for Gerhard Richter)

1.

shapes of dream moving beneath

what tone what
tones black white grey

2.

windows smashed
row of windows
rows of windows
odd-shaped holes to look out of
faces appear in corners

hacked, smashed, blown
out of air
the mixture of
elements

she dyed her hair and
cut it, rearranged it
there are photographs to show this
"change of appearance"

one of the men had eleven
disguises
they are documented in
eleven photographs

the woman, Gudrun, was
arrested in a boutique
after a shop assistant
spotted her gun

cool air of the morning

all those dreams
apocrypha
the night just as it was, but
out of that

bullet in the arse

Shining back, flowing back
meditative face, the
high cheek-bones, long face
tight but lovely line of the lips
toughness
lines of the neck

she was found dead in her cell

another was shot in the eye
by police

"A time (he said) is quickly approaching

the eye the eye

"when the privilege of immunity for the
"crimes of the ruling class

lines of the neck

"and their henchmen…
"will disappear…"

"News is sold as a commodity, information
"as a consumer product

the target in the wind, the lines
of force

"– what's not consumable must make them
"vomit"

3.

each night
wet with thin rain

for those who pass in
and out of the rooms
one room the tree
in near-dark

How the ethical gazes out
irrevocable, from iris and pupil

Thesis

…of stories. Thought, itself, ruptured. Dreams interpreted by one prisoner for another. Their confessions heard hurriedly in corridors, while awaiting interrogation.

•

They walked to a park just at the edge of the town, and sat down on a bench together. He was too distressed to understand much of what his friend was saying, uttering no more than a monosyllable now and again in response. One sentence of his friend's detached itself and remained, and through it a man walked in and put on a pair of dark glasses before entering a hospital ward for the dying.

•

A procession of like and unlike images. Those that are unlike are more appropriate, he said, being consistent with negation.

•

So many times, conversing with friends before waving goodbye beside water. Now, by a river you stop still, with your fears and longings held in a skein. Wavering, promising exchange: the boundary-line of breath and shadow.

•

A young woman sits on a wall in an attitude of waiting, dangling her legs; she smokes a cigarette, occasionally turning her head from side to side. She waits there with thoughts affectionate and generous to some fault; thoughts that are ringed with loneliness. This occurs as part of a story whose record is at once diary and dream. An alien and tender caress lies within its turnings.

A blessing performed? – By a drunken woman in a train carriage. (She'd earlier brushed against the young woman, apologising and then apologising again, for taking a drink straight from the bottle. – I'm excusing myself to you, she said, because you're a lady; but I wouldn't to anyone else.)

•

I go to meet my image, the liturgy says; and as if you were returning from a prison, your image comes to meet you.

(Dear M.,
 What I would want to say is that one places oneself in the present (there is nowhere else to be), in the spirit of someone attempting to retrieve or recover what has become obscured. And in order to do this – or <u>in the process</u> of doing so – one disrupts or ruptures the flow, the continuity, of time, narrative, history...)

•

As with ends, so with origins: a gnome to read, recite? He would recite, sing and unfold story after story folding back into other stories. – No one way, he said, of relating how things happened. Push everything back as far as it will go, there's still something to say. *So listen...*

•

A stranger, visiting, tells a story that intertwines with other stories, confuses its own beginnings, and jars the heart. Somewhere in its folds are a man and a woman in rags, who address each other as royalty while the man's seated on a dung-heap and the woman dances before him. – The story's for wisdom's sake, the stranger says.

I dream of a river by a field.

Suite

She ran past me on the bridge, then slipped to the ground in a sprawl, helpless. Her friend, running in pursuit, called out your name; and, having caught up to her, sat down beside her to give comfort. How well it could have been you: eclipsing your own control; wilful against concern.

·

Sitting on a small chair, out of the heat; writing in a notebook.

Looking through a sequence of gaps, holes.

·

– At first you seemed to relate to the other things going on in the room, but later you became blasé. – I've never been blasé in my entire life, I said.

·

Water's suspended, rippling, against the ceiling's extent.

An employment of failings, faults. A broken writing.

·

She told me how he was in the habit of following her in the street, and that she'd once started running and been chased by him. There was also an occasion, at a party, where it was necessary for several people to restrain him when he saw her about to leave with another boy. Yet she encouraged his friendship, even thinking of him as a close and exceptional kind of friend. After they'd lost track of each other, she asked for my help in locating him.

.

Within the haze-fire: a stillness. Divorced.

A blue cupola supported by trees.

.

– If you outlive your contemporaries, he told me, you get to establish your own version of what happened. But what really counts is the way that losses come to inform your writing more and more.

The London/Hartgrove Notebook

(for Ian McKeever)

Death's a limit to time, imprinting the air. Through exhaustion, he'd renounced *all the apprehensions of his understanding*. A shade of black, he said, *warm*.

He advised me: Don't write about people you know – unless you've told them you're doing it. As we walked up and down the island quay together, he related a story about his youth, and then said: I'm going to ask you never to repeat this. I forgot the story within days.

*

Sitting on bare floorboards, listening to the resonant guitar sounds: a gospel song, *Great Dreams from Heaven*, graciously slow.

Or walking together along the narrow streets leading down to the harbour. His speech – not as rhetoric, but as necessity – was veined with negation; mine, with longing.

.

The talk shifts away from the image of an antechamber where powers are to be cajoled or commanded for one's own earthly gain.

(…)

– Tell me, how did it begin?

– It began with a death. A death is always the beginning.

Lying down in the hotel room, I dreamt of various pieces of evidence that were presented to me one by one, each of them inscribed accordingly.

The surrounding walls were taped along the extent of their numerous cracks. A dictionary lay open on the table, with the word "fissure" circled in ballpoint.

•

Angelology disposes the proximity of swords and of eyes. – A deflection from the voice that announces, startles, enlightens.

The miniaturist, intent on the small white flowers, is overtaken by the collapse into starlight.

*

Stories that propose an intervention, the clarity of it shaking all else apart. Or so they're interpreted, as we talk in the front room of my friend's house, a small gathering; a landscape of hills and fields visible from the window.

•

This purity of event (I once wrote), *the drop of water, or milk, just that drop, in forming, attended to in a room.*

So my friend said nothing against me although I'd said I despised her; attending perhaps to what in the separation forms, over the hours until I call her again.

Different for her than for me although for both there is this drop, and there may be another.

*

My eyes don't have the auric flecking that gold injections sometimes, if rarely, cause.

They limn the saguaro's white flowers and red fruit; the face of the young woman who brushes her long hair, held bunched in one hand, against her own lips.

*

The angels hold torches, not swords or spears; admiration for the dead body vivid in their faces.

– Suspend the image as an inset, oneiric, in a text troubled by both defacement and effacement.

.

Word follows word as each sung note's placed, shaping the air; and we find ourselves attending to a story – such that the words themselves barely adumbrate. Sitting with my friend in his house on a Dodecanese island, we talked of Billie Holiday, and he told of having met her once in some small club, and of being invited to her place after she'd finished singing for the night. – I didn't go, he said when I asked for details; I had an essay to write for college the next morning.

*

And it all stopped, Will Petersen wrote. *He made corrections, corrected the sung syllables in terms of the dance. No, the song was not dark enough. When he closed his eyes and listened the song did not let him see.*

*

We came to the weeping beech, with its massed branches – twisted, pendulous, dense with leafage – making an enclosure of bizarrerie. The children preceded us, bending down under the low-lying boughs; going in to what in memory was a brooding quiet, a dark chamber.

.

No images were evident; we couldn't understand the language of what little dialogue there was, and for the rest the soundtrack was violent noise.

A thicket; thickets, one following another after another, a series seemingly without end.

*

By the cafés and stalls near the quayside a young woman sweetly dawdles; kohl around her eyes. Unforeseen gifts: carnations and sprigs of vervain.

Someone's been lost on the water, in fog.

*

In the way it provided exemplars, he said, it was an *ars poetica*, in pencil, ink; the lines varying in their darkness and breadth, velocity and weight.

.

The figure in black and light blue appears, epiphanic, from its ground (grey, broken by brown and green), as the ground appears with its figure; the image lifted from stone. As rocks are set within a rectangle of sand, the raked white expanse emerging with the rocks.

*

In the morning he received an obscene drawing from a woman he knew, a self-portrait caught within the capricious twists and entanglements of its lines. Roseate.

*

– To be known only through what's said in recrimination; or through the evidence of sorrow, hurt.

The woman saying to her teenage son, as they stood together on a station platform: I'd never in all my life have believed you could do this to me; then turning away, silent.

*

Sitting at a café table, the young woman's face is partially hidden from your gaze by a grille. If you were to sit at her table, you'd witness the drawing she makes with pastels on a blank postcard, endeavouring to locate what lies before her.

The little girl's poised at her school essay on a legendary singer, whose art was born of *all the contradictions*. The love songs a distillate, the initial *Ah* an admonition to tenderness.

(Untitled / for Bill Cirocco)

lakeside walk
light flickers

bird songs
tree psalms

white flakes
emerald

song or dream

------

lights cold light
water's flow

brilliance
negation

white flakes
darkness

eye and eye

the drift
beyond hotels houses

smitten
you break she said

the waves

the words
you break your word

awash

moving to the margins
of what an image can be then
crossed over and through
Hazard your erratic tracings
retracings have held my days
for months blessing

Derivation

"snow, trees   into abstraction
needle-points in the white
sliced into the surface
like chopping timber
with a sharp" love

long-sustained gazing her eyes
and his in lazy regard
and the curiously wry
slant of her tenderness
evident in every look

anything anything that it could be it
was disaster glimpsed
as a supernatural sign (Yugao)
(the love suicides at Sonezaki)

he spoke of prophecy's end
the vision made manifest
the things believed through love
present to the eyes the touch

he showed me his notebooks
read from them saying
they're a crystalline lattice
encompassing a rain of details

his mouth close to my ear
hissing: the obscurity
the face and the face
his spittle in my ear

we stopped at the sea –
an arcade
appearing & disappearing
as the tones of the voice build on the air

the surface, however, is always written.
my hands rest there
neither do they
attempt
description.

scratched
& the body too is marked,
en-
gendered.

a surface
where all this writing is,
beneath the words
a woman scribbles a black line heavily.

Power
        reproduces an image
of the heart
heartless:

        a magic
wheel, spokes
sticking in chest, back,
cheeks –

        image literal –
processional
spectacle
        (leaves on the
ground they walked;
colours
against the sky).

        Red – she spoke in
the room, standing at the window –
a favourite colour
        (red petticoat, beet-
root red).

        (Poor
people arranged themselves
by night's waters
in the heat,
hard by the narrow
dark streets.)

Wild Poignancy
Notes and Fragments (for Ian McKeever)

The clusters of twisted branches comforted me with the small splendour of their erratic design.

Searching for a face, through what occurs…. In distress: the doorframe a refuge.

    wild poignancy

Frederick Edwin Church: sunrise in the wilderness and a moonrise over the ocean (as allegories of his children's deaths from diphtheria).

    genesis / destruction
    life / death
    beginning / end

but:

    death / resurrection
    end / new and eternal life

House of light / house of darkness // house of darkness / house of light.

Waking to the night sky
(desert house)

Waking: a figure of stars seen through a glass wall.

Waking / stars waking

          stellar
          lustration
          lustrated
          glimpsing

…pouring out of spirit – dreams / prophecies / visions.

(Think of Jay DeFeo's painting *The Rose*, at times titled *The White Rose* or *Deathrose*. Eight years of painting and re-painting, building up and scraping back and building up, gluing pieces of wood and bits of jewellery to the surface and painting over them…. Vision realising itself through extraordinary persistence. When her friend Bruce Conner filmed the removal of this very large and extremely heavy artwork from DeFeo's studio, he called the film *The White Rose: Jay DeFeo's painting removed by Angelic Hosts*.
(The artist Wallace Berman photographed DeFeo standing in front of *The Rose*, naked and with arms outstretched and feet apart… the lines of her body echoing the lines of the painting.
(In another photograph DeFeo holds a partly shattered wineglass, filled with red rose petals.)

"But we all, with open face beholding as in a glass the glory of the Lord, are changed into the same image from glory to glory, *even* as by the Spirit of the Lord." (*2 Corinthians*, 3:18; King James Version.)

Interpretation (dreams, memories, texts)
      and the exhaustion / surpassing
            of interpretation (understanding).

          a spike fiddle
          passionate outpouring
          its sounds *scattering stars*

Glory – fire – cloud
Glory – Shekinah
Glory – goodness / grace / mercy

…I write, rewrite – for the sake of what remains invisible in the showing-forth.

Tracings, crossings, re-crossings / entrances, exits. Passing through / passing over.

Oskar Fischinger: "look into your eye, go down into your own eye – and going – ." Patterns of light. Going *into* the eye – or going *out* from the eye. Light threaded through, each to each. Eyes / face // eye-to-eye / face-to-face. (*Kenosis* in relation to a *going-out – other-directed*.)

> *threading light*
> *an envelope*
>
> gloriole

memory water flowing
floating faces up
and past
beside

the places
in memory a river flowing beside
the flow of people
here
through which
two photographs
smiling images

dear friend
I argue most with
two of you are placed
in what is a light
or a question

placed in the blessing
dark blue sky
and stars attached to an umbrella
held over the
blessing gesture

the sign of a question
yet here in instance
speaking your name
a man also
raises a blessing
which he moves into
to fall out of

a river flowing beside
the flower
the voice
two images smiling images
placed

placed in the blessing
question
dark blue sky
and stars

RELATION:

this morning
awoke late to rain

                        even if
it had not been

....

I sit in a café
drinking coffee
poor vagrant woman
sits down opposite
for shelter
yet without cup helpless
against the waiter's spite

....

walking away –

& behind me
whether the other's
footsteps
or the rain

I can't tell

....

"ironic" the return of another
to my own

a light goes on in the door
a note is sustained

....

released
out into the
street, dark, wet

as if in my room
alone.
walking towards

a gate of metal
bars, smooth, black
gleaming wet

....

each moment
is absence
the life
is past
& future
joined by nothing
this extraordinary
centre
ocean – how
do we come to know

3
  swings

(green, red, blue
seats)
        moving –

no children –

      in wind

someone (mother?)
falling down
in the street

....

as with my father
in childhood

I watch girls passing
along the platform
my father dead
thirteen years

tracks bending
into distance

....

father threw wheat
onto the roof
for pigeons & sparrows

as mother did too
— in his shadow
light

snow field
shadow tree

distress
affliction

station
or shelter

water to blood

stone and wood

in a corner
my own corner
sorrowing

                                              / shadow

                / glory

/ crosswise

Hagoromo

sorrow
for the
angel
robbed of
her robe
can't re-
turn to
heaven
and dies

- - -

or else
dances

Elegy

One evening we wandered one poorly lit street after another, lost in pouring rain. *Kind*, you said, and rightly, of the two young (very young) street-girls who eventually led us, in a small procession, to the main road.

.

Every now and again something's accomplished. (Names; commentaries.)

.

Marginalia to disjunction, as the lettering around the holes in the vellum seemed. (And the veining: brown-black from the brutality.)

.

Hell into heaven: as a light is switched off by a finger's flick. Gaze into the impossible egress.

.

Without hope, I follow the paths that appear and disappear in dream's indistinct weather.

.

Study shifts, transformations while water drips, domestic. Or flows, spills, splashes; gulls above in a cloud-filled sky.

.

A lyric elegy: the trumpet-player improvises on *Here's that Rainy Day*, against plucked double bass; a dialogue emerging from the solitary sounds.

The Book of the Spoonmaker

(for Tony Rudolf)

It's true I have dreams about non-existent books. The spoonmaker – who wasn't merely a spoonmaker, but that's easy to surmise – spoke against defining good in dependence to evil, as its opposite term. – The room, he wrote, is a trap for flares.

.

I opened the door; a young woman was sitting inside the room, writing. She looked up, astonished to see me there. I had no idea who she might be. She and I took stock of the fact that neither of us was an orphan and she wasn't a widow. (Nor indeed had she ever been married.) On the other hand, we were both from a distant country.

.

The paintings and drawings were acknowledged to provide only limited and fragmented documentation of a special history. I would have liked to have thumbtacked the images to the walls and walked round them with her, one by one; for I wanted to hear what each revealed to her. – You persist in writing about art, when you're supposed to be writing about all manner of other things! And your characters – they *always* discuss subjects that real people hardly ever talk about! I dream of being denounced by breakfast waiters in front of several of my friends.

.

From childhood: a fear of running molten metal, or the sudden din of machinery. We threw our drinks at each other, caught up in a drunken hilarity. At one point my friend gestured towards our host and exclaimed: I think this guy's the Devil! The artist began to write around then over his drawings and paintings. He'd taken the young woman round a private view of another artist's work, loudly denouncing every exhibit with splenetic verbal pyrotechnics.

.

I do end up writing about art, in one sense or another, in most of my work. In divergence, it needs to be said. – What else, she asked, did the spoonmaker say? He said he wanted to redefine empathy in the light of the willingness to be shaken, ruptured, self-abnegated in one's engagement with another person. Meaning and art, he said, could be understood in the wake of such a displacement or dispossession.

.

In Franck's oratorio of the Beatitudes, the despairing thinker is included among those who mourn, together with the orphan, the widow and the stranger. The procession of figures was seen as through tinted glass, the colours shifting between one portion of glass and the next. Locutions were summoned and dissolved by grief. We'd taken the steep path that led up the hill to the castle, my friend insisting upon photographing me at various points along the way. When we were coming back down, I was overtaken by a dizzying, sickening impulse to throw myself from the hillside into the sea below.

.

My friend and I went in search of him and found him in bed, lost to a blissful, drunken sleep. No amount of talking, shouting, prodding or shoulder-shaking served to rouse him. The door wouldn't open to our tugging and pushing; and the keys I found in a leather jacket by the bed didn't fit the lock. (When my friend returned from searching the rest of the boat, he informed me that it was his own jacket.) Finally, when we were close to giving up, my friend discovered that the door opened by sliding sideways.

———

…yellow, blood-coloured, violet, water-coloured, and grayish-black. Walking on the bridge at midnight, we found ourselves overtaken by shouts and exploding lights and the noise of glass being broken. The young woman's hand on my arm was the single locus of revocation.

•

Avenues of ivy-covered trees between the long rows of gravestones; pebbles placed on the graves, in remembrance. By divergence: the need, the spoonmaker wrote, to be emptied of oneself. In transverse imitation of the divine exemplar. The anagogical is a limit that presupposes supplementary levels, he also wrote.

Stromata

Book One

Sitting on a coil of rope, he watched the man fall asleep on a map large as a blanket. The map tore with the man's turnings; pieces were blown into the dark waters.

.

– There was a painter who lived in an island hut, painting at night by a dimly lit kerosene-lamp.

– Almost in darkness…

– He didn't look at the paintings in the daytime. And when he saw them exhibited in galleries…

– Under artificial lights…

– …he'd often denounce them as forgeries.

.

Standing at the sea's edge, waiting for the rain to break, I think of that day we walked together along the mudflats by the river.

She sang the melody without any embellishment; her voice "true", drawing the lines of song through the air.

There was a plant fragment (polypody) caught in her hair. – Don't move, I said; just for a moment.

.

– Figures of infinite regress bore me but *not* him.

I caught the sentence and missed its meaning, my attention more on other things: the fire that had been built from planks and branches; the wine being passed around in paper cups; the two little girls wrapped in their blue sleeping-bags, both girls white-faced after a dip in the cold night sea.

.

A man tells his companion of rituals involving fire and binding (knots, webs). The girl is small and thin; in her middle teens. The man's older. They walk over a bridge, down a narrow walkway, then another walkway; it's dark and there's a strong wind, and this entire riverside area appears empty of other people. She says to him, laughing, Is this where you turn into a monster, now? He walks away from her. She shouts, Bastard, fuck you! but the man, already at some distance, in the gloom beyond the streetlamps' reach, doesn't answer. She shouts again, her voice tearing: Is it over, then?

.

Not even the reed-mats' lines, white powder of decayed material; nor the smashed adornments of *the small princess* – fragments of gold decorations belonging to one so young that her death left her unaccompanied, entailing none of the sacrificial killings familiar to the excavators.

A perfected abandonment.

The eye sees stone, and sees nothing. The wall is quite literally a wall, to which the young woman presses her face, her body shaking as she weeps.

.

During a holiday abroad, my friend sent me a postcard about seeing a film at an open-air cinema, *to the accompaniment of jets landing at the nearby airport, and with the underwater photography mostly washed out by poor projection and too much extraneous light.*

He returned; and one evening we stood together and talked, in the small garden at the back of his house, while the darkness settled. He spoke of the long illness and death of a mutual friend of ours: before these events, he said, it had seemed that similarity, even uniformity, had been most important to him – in persons as much as in nature.

.

Dear –,
    It was too quick for a dream, nor was I asleep as I stood there, having closed the door behind me, and about to switch on the lights. For an instant, a girl was crouched in a corner, sobbing.... And when the lights were on, and I saw that the room was empty, a voice, only just audible, kept calling my name. It was if the pain you'd related of your adolescence, twenty years in the past, suddenly woke in me. Coulisses? Nothing in the room took on such an aspect; there was nothing there by which I could save myself.

.

A man sits in the dark; listening, nostalgically, to a recording of nature sounds. I don't; I think of a friend, a much-admired older poet. I think of when we sat talking in a café near his hotel; and of how later that day I wandered alone through a park, trees uprooted from the storm of two nights before, each thought of his voice breathing calm upon the air around me. The very sound in memory was my refuge.

Book Two

Sitting beneath the almond tree in blossom, I watched a little girl, the delight in her face simple and frank, skipping the rope held by another girl and an old man.

The dark came, and with it the lighting-up of the streetlamps bordering the park.

(Later:) I listen to Chet Baker singing *Imagination* and *My Foolish Heart*, the voice tender in its candour. *Colour so fragile…* it seems *as if it could be blown away.*

.

– …and did you know that your painter crossed the Timor Sea on a raft, starved and hallucinating at the end of the voyage, his obituary already printed?

But those and other details about him had been with me for many years; and I'd once written:

> A lone man on a raft
> crosses a Sea. Imaged face
> becomes almost the shape
> of a paper lotus-petal –
>
> we remember the dead with prayer
> and dream, equally those we love
> who will die. Paper lotus-petal:
> flickering lines across its surface.

.

She stretched over the couch where I was sitting, to pick up the glass of wine on the floor. The arch of her back, the small nakedness between blouse and skirt. In the vertigo born of an upsurge of longing, sight momentarily emptied itself out. – Between her writing desk and mine: so many ways of saying. (Sitting together at a table in the flat that belonged to her absent friend, she'd read her poems to me from the characters that appeared on the small dark blue screen. Her voice composed the details of a mimesis *derived*, as Gadamer says, *from the star-dance of the heavens.*) – And if I look up to see threads of snow falling in my room, like the sea that Su Tung-p'o woke to, where his floor had been…?

.

I was working for a time in a late night bookshop, located – curiously – in a seedy garment district. I was there once during a storm, reading and listening to the rain and the long rolls of thunder, when an acquaintance came through the doorway, dripping water onto the floor.

– Beware young women who believe they're in contact with statues, he said. – A gift for delusions, he continued; sitting in that museum day after day, communing with the damn things.

Looking out the window, I remembered:

>   …blood soaks into the carpet
> under bare feet

– but not thinking of him. – There was a window in the poem, with two people standing at it.

>   …What sea
> have we come to, it strikes
> the smallest thing: *the radiant heart.*

.

You leaf through the book, looking at the way the colours of the letters are displaced, black by red, for pages…. Misery's singular, however many the lives it possesses; and though assigned to marginalia, its images impoverished, powerless – it claims me in you, claims succour: and I am claimed utterly; so that I take place through this dispossession.

.

– I dreamt I took my children's bones from their graves, washed them, fondled and kissed them… and I awoke raving, with the sun.

– But you don't have any children, I said.

– Yet there was something…, he said; something that held me.

(He'd seen my friend waiting at the bus-shelter, in a memory borrowed from a single photograph; whereas I, long familiar, was rendered invisible.

(Sitting in the disused bear-pit, my two companions and I drank to the spirits – we said – of the dead bears. Later, we saw the remains of the old rheumatology clinic, now mere rubble. And following a path isolated in light, came to a mausoleum covered with scratched inscriptions, the angels' faces mutilated.)

○

A friend writes: I'm sitting here, out of the heat, thinking about what you've written regarding the human image. How could one *ever* be able to paint another person, I've asked myself….

Another friend: We lift the groups of bones, with the earth in which they're found, as one mass – which is then encased in a layer of plaster of Paris.

– *Dream folding into waking life and back into dream, and within those folds, the strands of yourself tearing apart.*

○

Dear –,
  If I think of what is most terrible in a life, the life of someone I love, it is almost entirely unsayable. Unless it is a matter of testimony, how can you say it? Let alone write about it: for personal histories are not "usable"; even though they may be drawn upon, if respect and reticence are the keys to a distinction.

My sister wrote to me, Do you still paint? I hope you do, because you are too good to stop. The picture of a girl with red hair you did in pastel is lovely. – Not only had I stopped – I couldn't remember any such picture; nor even working in pastels. But whatever the medium of portrayal, I can only approach the idea of imaging another human being with something akin to fear....

Yet in what's said and written and shown, there is always this possibility: time itself called to judgment.

•

He pulled the large drawings out from beneath his bed to show me. Colour, as well as imagery, had been displaced. But I thought of Izutsu: *Black here is not sheer black. For in its negation of all colours, all colours are positively affirmed.*

This man, the artist, works in daylight; I write in the evenings. I like to think of Rilke, when he was Rodin's secretary, writing at night, the lamp in his window signifying work done in the night; and the young Cocteau seeing that light, but not knowing for many years that it was Rilke who'd occupied the room.

Moments

Graph of durations: grid on which we move. Cut each line on the grid down, down to where thought stops. *When a line is cut into many parts, no matter how many the parts, something will be left. One can never cut into the last unit.*

•

"The hare will never conclude the race which is his love – each moment is divided, cut down further, closer to impossibility. He runs and is still." Ah yes; my hand reaches toward you, reaches and will not reach. Yet even in the photograph, how evident that water has already bathed the wound.

•

Perhaps it's that very moment when the child raises her head, with its shock of auburn hair, to look up at the sky; a look that's immediately cancelled by the sun's too-intense brightness.

Or perhaps it's another selection of time, not an afternoon's blue, but a dawn completely red, orange. Cry out in the midst of it.

Messages

The corona in this dark is your being's (mouth pressed tenderly upon mouth). Sending a kiss, I duplicate the sign of unlettered identity.

·

The shapes of interpretation rise up at the borderline between stasis and flux. I trace the oppositions and equations, negations and similitudes; my hand does not cease in the labour.

·

In the stops and breaks of her story, the evening concentrates her glances; her young voice edging towards maturation, tells me in clear tones, "I disappeared from all their lives then", *tabula rasa* which the circulating lines of desire trace, and trace over, and over.

·

Daylight hours were spent asphalting the roads and streets. Black ink ideograms filled the rest of the time: reversed to white in the heart's dictation.

·

What is it which we, looking at each other, can only translate, imperfectly, into longing – into words expressive of longing? – Unity; which is not "beyond good and evil", but rather the "beyond" of good and evil – the transcendence implicit, positively, in good – as its fulfilment; and in evil – as its negation.

·

As in a dream: knowledge bleeds into foreknowledge of fresh atrocities; the dead walk back into corrupt skins, telephone their orders of butchery again.

.

– If you've gathered the flames about you and locked the doors, to die with your signs: how bitter the ecstasies then.

– Melodrama isn't extinguished in café small talk – in its so-ordinary semi-darkness; but in the victims' insistent claim to be heard.

So he seemed to say; and so I thought; and we talked around these things, sitting in a café, looking out at the columns of piled stones in the street.

.

Looking out or looking in: the portico and the door and window are flames. Hands gesture in talk, the fingers spread; the voice catches; and the face, given into my life, endures.

(From:) The Preparation

eight hours' exposure
for the single photograph:
between dark & light
there is the duration of looking there,
the definition of consciousness
is that of death:
the day you conceive of your birth
you also define your death,
the stone stands up in the light, your body
speaks.

.

alone.
the boat. "I"
waiting   the words come
back, they will come back.
prepare the tongue
& the body
for the celebrations,
"of the conjunction of Male & Female
"of their copulation
"of the philosophical conjunct of man & woman.
"of the black tincture;
"buds appearing in the glass
"of the red colour."

.

gate / section
the stones, violently blond, overexposed
& the gymnasts appear, frozen in motion

in their incredible poses in the air.
moon / white brick
the park at night, folded
into the texture of the soil itself.
sound of walking through
dry leaves, with the voices
not quite coming through, voice
of the physics lecturer, continuing
into the park in daytime.
the mouth black frame & white frame
the penis

 .

40 windows. by means of a rapid flickering
or rippling movement through which an essentially static
image passed *flame / snow*
causing a tension to exist between *energy / speed*
& *duration / slowness*, the window cuts through the night,
beating violently.

 .

double
at the street's edge
(afterglow around the limbs).
it is a search
in mentality
where mentality doubles
irresistibly.   that I *want,*
want, sucking / drawing up on air
on the blue air. body-mass
my sexuality liquefies
the grains of dialogue spread & mingle.

 .

I walked the streets at night
like seeing my alter ego there.
wine
the signature visible without writing or
saying anything.
the sudden fits of laughter destroy the world.
shifting
from one to the other.
our letters, our voices, continue into each other,
a blue line in the branches of the tree.
the letters (the voices) continue. they do not "reach"
they continue.

.

map of *presence*,
the body (the image) spliced into radiance,
the durations spliced into radiance,
words & colours
shifted. the markings on the stone,
the light in the pupils of the eyes –
it changes (and that
it changes): the light
in the stone,
the changing light.

.

love considered in terms of an acoustic instrument (the voice).
techné of that instrument, &
of others,
made with the hands.
air, earth, fire, & water. the
resonances
& interactions.
the body is made,

sounds resonating deep
in every organ. you feel
the shape & extent of every organ. each & every organ
of the body.
Roscoe Mitchell's saxophone solos.

The Story

friendliness and love.
the mirror. the streets
a thickness, a mirror.

the story
in the street,
in the street to have
more than the one work
on the go at any time.

the horizon.
the story that stops and goes
on again. the heart

.

on a motorcycle from the station
through the snow
to this page.

the snow, heaped.
the heart

.

– was it the word PLENUM
you had on the tip of your tongue?

– MILK, you said, the milk
splashing on your wrists.

.

a building in Holloway, which seems to me one of the most beautiful I have ever seen: simple in structure, a very simple brick building, but painted in the most joyous colours and figurations, like a kid's notion of Easter or Bob Lax's notion of the Circus: "Once more now they are with me, golden ones, / living their dream in long afternoons of sunlight; / riding their caravans in the wakeful nights".... the building has been boarded up and surrounded by tin fencing, so that you can only see the top of it clearly. this is, I suppose, to keep squatters or drunks out. possibly the painting of the building, which has brought its true life into the open, was done by squatters who have since been evicted.... in any case the building seems set for demolition.

·

through
your eyes
the line (dash)

in fact. (I will call you.)

the line from your eyes.

·

at this point:
viola music.

·

building a house is what any man or woman
desires. note by note,
the structure takes hold and moves on.
it is a relationship. the only City.

.

you move forth into a society of loves

it designs the world and the world pulls up short.
just at that point.

.

the spaces
are shot through with music.
the City. the stones against the horizon.
shot
silk.

.

I cut each note down. it was so fast.
the perception was so fast. each perception

children swinging on ropes, jumping on and
swinging, as described as theme.

.

you and I, we, already exist
in this work. it has no doors.
we already exist in it.

without too great a fuss
we have taken possession
of the Restaurant and Cabaret of West Europe
and we sing, eat and drink to your health.

.

this place.

the music
is to be played:
modestly and vivaciously,
in a singing voice,
with slight modulation of dynamics,
without cessation of attack.

it is played.

o

      almost
to shine.

drunkenness.
puking in the gutter outside the pub.

fire –   fire –
in that brief time they take to step outside –

everything planned in advance.
Russia: Kronstadt.
not formation, but
design.

.

each unit. so slow.
the perception so slow. each
perception.

children swinging on ropes, leaping,
swinging, as described as theme.

.

that story was the story you told,
a curve
as notation for music.

to question the term "unit" is to
question the term "totality"
and I question it.
no one knows what is meant by
                              "perception".

.

today a friend told me about an aged Russian woman he once knew, who was literally seized with terror if someone was introduced to her as a "Trotskyite"; she remembered friends murdered at Kronstadt.

.

order and chance:
two flimsy concepts.

the line of the text.
it is that elbow that swings
to the sea, the blueness,

it is that
line:
your arm, my arm.

.

we already exist in this work.
it is not context. there is no containment.

a wilderness.
a house.
a City.
in the work our faces (and the faces of our friends)
assume a reckless humour,
I
love them, the glass
floods with light.

.

the percussion stops dead.
your beauty –
flitting across the floor in your bare feet.

it is almost laughable,
the blood.

.

the work's inner movement
pulls us into the present;
illuminating the possible.
I pull on the rope,
the words
        interminable,
scarred,
just there where the ghosts dance.

.

drag me into the sunlight,
you say.
is this brutality?

I watch while
they drag you.

·

that place
is to kick against
                 like it kicks
like remembrance,
fire that burns my hand
to ashes
and gives each page of my writing
its entrance and disappearance.

or rather it is co-extensive with
each page,
the story in which "I love you"

·

eyes and tongue and skin
lick in
little points of moisture
and little lights.
the bright and dark tones
both electric.

the windows. duration.
I feel such fear when I see you,
which is *perfect* description.
yellow grass
and laughter.

gaps, gaping holes, perfectly formed,
in the flow of water.
within the spiral of numbers
love could reach such a speed
we'd know each other instantaneously
and from all time. forgiveness
for believers and unbelievers.
this is the City, that I am facing you.

The Music

1.

a balance
informing the series
manifestation and absence

porcelain basin
window above it
ceiling above that

friendship (gold) separation
(no colour)

a road in light of evening
nearing Easter
a stairway
a room
a figure leaning in the doorway
head leaning against
description which draws near
one hand held up
veils

2.

a series of rectangles
maybe a pavement
maybe not a pavement

intersections (grid)
durations

point unison
belief

now stain now glow
now fire

floor wall ceiling

grass stone

street house
sky

3.

red neon light on wet flagstones
my image in the shop window
part window-glass part mirror
traffic-lights and cinema beyond

doorway offer of hand another doorway
one following the other into a room
another again into a room another room
different occasion standing in the doorway

unison the movements their structure
lady of veils
water a lake a river a bridge

4.

the movement
out of time *Mystic Nativity*
refusal of humanism
in scale of figures
the movement upwards

the one (the human) embraced
(the angelic)

attention adoration birth
the onlookers the mother the child

blue sky above it gold vault
circle of figures whirling ecstatic

5.

a garden a café
a grove of orange trees

the movement across
the surface
left to right
light moving across

a movement
to read
a movement
to be sung

a yearning
arc of fire from the rim
of the sun
imprints lunar equal

6.

I had forgotten
the three kneeling figures

who might have been
in former life

the Graces
whose dance also is gone

here into that motion of figures
at the ceiling

an abandoned room
light flashing in an otherwise darkness
time momentum the house
the music

7.

a grove of orange trees
a silence in the midst
of music
shy and gentle one

shy gesture love's
personification
avenue with trees

orange a window a street
a room
a woman waiting in a grove

shift of meaning the lines intersect
unison
belief

red wine / light on wet flagstones
a pool of rain on the street
avenue trees
a lake a bridge

Primavera

1.

that I loved them, & that meant
loving them forever a small window
that for me it would be an *eternal*
memory
lost a darkness utterly black
travel no visible record

2.

so this is *image* poetry? he asked
no I said the voices faded in
afternoon air noise of traffic
early heat
I walked with my back to him
away into the crowd then turned
to face him he had already stopped filming

3.

white chalk on a blackboard
blue chalk on a blackboard
green chalk on a blackboard
yellow chalk on a blackboard
white blue green yellow
chalk on the pavement

4.

those children will take your hand
because unable to tell you
lead you away

they may kiss your mouth
to stop your commands
they will avoid your eyes then perhaps
stare fixedly into them
& then not look at your eyes again

5.

light changing the features
right side of the face
I mean, scarcely visible in reproduction

6.

the telephone the small window
table
no words
a gap at the heart of things
black space exactly next to
the light from the window

7.

"looking into" someone's face
then hearing their words over the telephone
table centre of the room
diffused light of afternoon

8.

walking in the woods for miles
then coming into my room
beyond allegory beyond dreams
pavement the only guide
the figure stopped put her head to the window
looking out
her eyes pensive

9.

two figures (one my friend) their backs
both of them facing
that wall
the Wailing Wall
a death

10.

a wood a forest my own youth
city material images of high contrast
footsteps through a doorway to follow the differences
in how we walked
between some fragments O light of Spring

Insistence

the orders
ascending
descending

scale of light

•

came to the room
where he slept
remembering the cold
of the night
(the cold
of the snow)

came to cover him

but stopped
in the dark
looking across the space
as he looked
across the space

quite still

◦

based on lengths or durations
events   episodes
ascending and diminishing

◦

banal snow

trees

scale

•

speaking of the periphery
listening to music
in a room
four flights up

•

window bright yard
the image
we timed

•

in the shade
small crimson flowers
speckled the green
of grass
brown
of earth

•

grey slabs of pavement
detaching themselves
slowly or running together
as if
continuous the hawthorn
low to the ground
its large and ordered shape
green leaves white flowers
red

•

I scarcely dream
at all
and the two nights
riddled
with dreams

•

the insistence
the spirit
small white flowers
she recalled
the names

they come out
on the streets

Voice

1.

how placed
to such understanding
are you, or I
how placed with the
traffic
and the shadows of the
buildings

the *voice* of such
which is a persistent
rain
a few trees pavement
then stone steps
in light

if you or I were to write here
"midnight sun" would it be
esoteric
would the phrase turn back
upon itself
into durance

how placed
that it is not academic
placed within the life

how placed
am I, or you?

2.

the society corrupt, alien-
ating,
yet even the children

(the story says)
recite the name of the holy
in the street as they play
name
itself foundation
ground, groundless
reaching as a voice
the pictures
the charm in the midst

3.

windows blur in
the image
from excess of light
                so
that only one edge
of four remains
as a clean straight line

rows of faces, some
of them sided with light

succession
flow maybe
of pictures, words
nothing within that
in itself to give love's solace

the discrete
frames of vision
the material
the transcendental
equally
a house
the boards fall
into the darkness
once more, speaking to

in front
sitting within that same
darkness
several

4.

a white nimbus
behind his head
like a dining-plate
gentle figure
receiving alms
above him against the night
are held white flowers
or stars

that night I dreamt
they had killed a monk
for wearing his robes the wrong way

a young boy's throat
slit
as an object lesson
he sprawled and writhed
in his own blood
helpless
we were
the periphery
seeing through
into nothing
groundless ground

(for Liz Thomas)

Children

1.

there was
light at the door,
the primary sign
or how the voice was,
disguised:

process of colour separation
which
brings us

the house occupied in fear of
being taken away again,
theme of *property*,
to paint the door red
and invite the night
                          breath
which begins the process,
across the park which
dips momentarily
until the voice appears

2.

the blackboards laid flat on the ground and
the figurations disrupted,
children
jump the numbers

ash on our faces and
theirs
we came here
the technique known as "jump-cutting"
(which can be distinguished from "spilling")

to achieve
the wedding celebrations

for which she cooked
in a house in her joy

(moussaka or lasagne)

3.

people merge
she is the *one* person,
moving

moving as the piano part remains
where it is

where she is, the district that
is her voice
breaking at the fountain
of her joy
the schema,
lines of varying THICKNESS

and the night sky entirely white

4.

tent-show trumpeters and circus rings
the actual world is the possible
extent
the possible world the actual
storm / thunder
and the language so funny, so ridiculous
that it is *ineffable*
soaked in the rain, trousers
rolled up

won from
a small heat
a concentration of warmth
to oppose
bodily
in the movements of the limbs

which is a change of colour

Moments

(i. m. –)

The monk
persisted, "Then, following
the universe, will the self

perish?" Daizui replied, "Like
all the rest, it will follow &
depart"

      walk forward a little, smiling

•

in that brief time taken to step outside
                    colour retained as trace

•

Space structured in the mind
& eye
as if in a dream

a field of grass
a piano

•

red wine soaks the grass
a deep
a moment

runs
air
eye

one square of grass
one, another, one

little girl, small space
– a dream of trees,
of flowers,
bushes also

across air, grass

the tides
a field of grass

one square of grass
& another perfectly adjacent
one
one

The little girl runs
runs fast now
The mother's eye

.

the sudden detail, perception
started to dry herself, to

runs fast now
& the eye? is
how fast? to show us that she was
dead / the smells of flowers: roses, hibiscus, jasmine

a gate, and that small concrete path
afterwards: coda

"the two different worlds: the real &
the unreal   For the sake of visual argument
I accepted the collage sections as a kind of reality"

"but in the final result, this hypothesis was of very
little importance"

Pictures of Mercy

(for Jackie Wray)

1.

Absence throws an image
into the doorway, her
voice to call out name

She kissed me
left cheek & right
in that pure space

Holes in the street
everywhere
recurring
one to
the other

2.

Walking a road
in starlight,
coming to a crossroads

*No time elapses,
no days
intervene*
This night, this
time –
the lake seen from one
corner to the other, a further
view
appearing where
she was

She said:
you are the source
of love, by your
very nature;
without the essence
the forms are
meaningless

Roses the length
of the fence,
pine, cypress, oak,
elm & willow,
mulberry & ash,
clouds & forests, hills
& rivers –

outbursts of crying
& over-
whelming
feelings

3.

Loving-kindness comes to where
I sit, sits down,
her thigh against mine –
asking, why did you stare
at me that way? I could
feel your
eyes

Where can they take
hold of rest, they look
from eyes to street, a stream
of people: of each, passing (the faces
chimeric)
she asked me, what
do you think you
would want to know?

4.

Waiting – an inter-
section length-
ening
shadow –

a table in
open
air
under branches
or branch

Participation

the plenum
striking
the hour, the image

mountain, field, moonlight
horses chomping grass

people inside a house sitting
on boards
talking

efforts each
to each arising
in which infinity

Plenum

the bridges
acacia trees
wild mimosa
we were
white

....

this last crisis

journey

....

burnt grass and stone
music twisting
beneath

....

in all

thread
fountain
guiding-line

....

a cold wind
drenching rain

diverted to television
it rains and rains
that lovely peninsula

nearer her

....

to echo

and

gift
full

for Elizabeth Lutyens

Participation

for ninety minutes
your voice
on the telephone
into early morning
my friend

....

a room
existing out of solitude
a room
a house
a City
destroyed
in this
O Grace

....

images thrown
(projected)

the levels
distributed
throughout

arrangement
incline to frame
transcendental

all the time
as if this
room were a street
& I was walking
to follow

....

streetlamps' light
shadows
chalk-markings
(children's games)

plenum
in time
slow
constant
changing within itself
constant
the mirage
the true image
pursuit
a flight of birds
a flight

....

neither details
nor
the whole
our beneficence

the body naked
the dream
between two hearts
waking
this life

Understanding
for Jackie

— this purity
of event
the drop
of water
or milk,
just that
drop,
in forming,
attended to
in a room

— so my friend
said nothing
against me
although I'd said
I despised her;
attending perhaps
to what
in the separation
forms
over hours
at night
until I call her again

— differently
for her
& for me
although for both
there is
this drop
& there may
be another

— "the more we transgress
the more let us trust"
"for only out of such trust
does a mind of tenderness

& forbearance
spontaneously issue"
& I must say
how lovely she is
in attendance
for it is not trust
in "chance" or "fate"
"destiny" or "coincidence"
or even "life"

— through the dark streets
of Covent Garden
in a slight rain
hurrying
for my other friend's play
which originally
we'd have gone to
together

— I must think this out
that an art
or a "wisdom"
which at any point
tries to exhibit
the actual being
as object
or as subject
is false
to participation

— a room
given over
to the social
to the aesthetic
or to cult
is not the room
"Lumen Gloriae" mis-
translated
"Glorious Light"

for "Light of Glory"
but the room
will need no preparations
we are already there

suddenly
there was

a tree in light
(or sapling,
rather –)
& it said
your name

there in the garden
five years ago,
it
called to you.

and I stopped, how long

to draw up the image
raise it, beloved face
in absence –

liquid image –
quicksilver –
eyes the eyes in passing sustain

so this night   you
were there
to turn into my recognition
speaking my name

for this I write –
the suddenness of your life
in streets & rooms

1969

(for John Riley)

We stood at the gate.
The husband was
inside, a violent patch
of dark red somewhere. She
was not less beautiful than
my memory. The path
was where we had come down;
the sun's strong light where we stood;
the calm – ? It was already
a dated scene; neighbours – two men –
sitting on their lawn; and she
smiling

We were on the path; there was anger
in me, that this
last time
would be the last time:
the patterns moving or still,
shadows, and the moving
in or out of shadows
on the grass.

Somewhere a man stood, a
speculation. His shadow
like an oak. I knew where she was
when I turned, at the gate, and
how beautiful. I knew that the
light was falling in the same
way

What Determines What We Are
(for Paul)

after I had
you had to
(sat down)
something you'd
thought important
I just *couldn't*
trying to explain
to leave
sense, because
left empty
by her or
to wipe away
the classic
and
simply be
involved
like them
if only
right here
to happen?
been brought
bound together
and more
to see what
things, is
what's done
other contact
particular
resembling
love, be
scnt, burned:
rags
the acrid
smoke
the
letters

all things
veiled
by its
in some
that I sense
to murder

of opposites
to that harmony
you used

every place
invisible
may be
for
a little
a moment
walking
the
real
that seeing
had other
      contact
      by this
      would
      to be
      attraction

GLORIA

white surface	balcony wall, above the porch opposite my window
white surface serrated	(grooved; eaten into by black) next to the balcony
white surface	wall, not clean, mouldy even/ light of a cloudy day
white surface	same; row of houses across the road from my room
white surface	same; row
white surface	same; row
white surface	same; row
white surface	same; row
white surface	same; row that my eye will not count past at this distance
black surface	streaked with white/ broken by glass (dark); door of the first house, same row
black surface	door, next along in row, but clearer (more purely black)
black surface	tilted, shining (hence uneven, hence more revealing of tilt) roof of same row, wet with rain
black surface	same
black surface	same (more even; less reflection of light)
black surface	same (less reflection again)
black surface	same (but even less reflection) the other roofs obscured from here
black surface	dull (grey-black) window of house opposite (nothing seen within) no vertical cross-piece
black surface	next window; same except narrower
white surface	wall, not clean, mouldy even/ light of a cloudy day
black surface	streaked with white/ broken by glass (dark); door of same house
black surface	tilted, shining (hence uneven, hence more revealing of tilt) roof of same house, wet with rain
white surface	next house in row
black surface	door of same house, clearer than the first (more purely black)
black surface	roof of same house
white surface	next house in row
black surface	roof of same house (more even; less reflection of light)

white surface	next house in row
black surface	roof of house (less reflection than with last roof)
white surface	next house in row
black surface	roof of house (even less reflection) the other roofs obscured from here by their chimneys
white surface	next house in row
white surface	next house in row; my eye will not see past this house from where I sit.

3 children
with a tricycle
one corner (far)
of the playground

park
one child (girl)
on a tricycle
with her mother

3 children (2
boys, one older girl)
running
down the street

2 little girls
with their mother
one girl running
a little ways,
the mother running
with her, the other
girl
walking behind

one little girl
crossing the road
a long scarf around
her neck
a large red bag
in her hand

2 women in the
park with
several small
children

Chris, his daughter Sarah and I were in the East End, to do some filming. Were in the East End, to do some filming we came upon a drunk who'd collapsed on the pavement. Chris, his daughter Sarah and I we came upon a drunk who'd collapsed on the pavement Chris saw that he was still breathing, and went into a betting agency where he was able to talk the staff into phoning for an ambulance. A drunk who'd collapsed on the pavement Chris saw that he was still breathing today in the Strand I passed a girl stumbling along dressed in torn and dirty clothing, a red handkerchief perched precariously on her ginger-coloured hair. And went into a betting agency where he was able to talk the staff into phoning for an ambulance her face was dirty and bore marks of disease a red handkerchief perched precariously on her ginger-coloured hair.

white terrace house opposite red & blue T-shirts hanging from one of
    the windows

the room dark the house opposite darkened lights on in rooms
the room illumined the house opposite darker lights on in rooms I write
    beneath a light

flame at one window (fire in the room)
moon-like lamp hanging at another

flame at one
hanging at another

window (fire in the room)
moon-like lamp

February 21 1977, Mathias sent me a postcard on the reverse side of which he thanked me for telling him about a Spanish translation of Chris Jones' book *Design Methods*. On the front side was a photograph of an Alpine scene, with criss-crossing ski-tracks and the figure of a skier in the foreground. Mathias had made a sketch in biro over top of the skier and the space around him, sketching what looks like a marriage of sculpture and architecture (something he has been doing for at least two decades, with various experimental buildings and sculpture-environments). I have it with me still. February 21 1977, Mathias sent me a postcard thanking me for telling him about Chris Jones' book *Design Methods*. On the other side of the card was an Alpine scene, with ski-tracks and a skier in the foreground. Mathias had drawn an architectural sculpture over the place where the skier had been (you could just barely see his form beneath the drawing). It was the type of thing Mathias has done for about two decades under the title of "emotional architecture". I have it with me still. February 21 1977, Mathias sent me a postcard telling me of his interest in Chris Jones' book *Design Methods*, which I'd mentioned in my letter of January 27. On the front side of the card was a colour photograph of an Alpine scene, with a skier and criss-crossing ski-tracks in the foreground. Over top of the skier and the space around him Mathias had drawn in biro a sculptural building. The biro marks leave the figure beneath them only barely visible, although from his red pullover Mathias has extracted a red bar or rectangle, an opening of some kind perhaps, which contrasts strongly with the predominant blue tonality of the photograph, even the white of the snow moving towards blue. The structure drawn into the landscape reminds me of similar work Mathias has done for over two decades, under the name of "emotional architecture". I have it with me still. February 21 1977, Mathias sent me from Paris a postcard telling me of his interest in Chris Jones' book *Design Methods*, which I'd mentioned in my last letter to him. On the front side of the card was a photograph of an Alpine scene, with a skier and criss-crossing ski-tracks in the foreground. Over the figure and his surrounding space Mathias had sketched a sculptural building, the sort of thing he has practised for at least two decades under the name of "emotional architecture". I have it with me still. February 21 1977, Mathias wrote to thank me for telling him about Chris Jones' book *Design Methods*. On the front side of his postcard was an Alpine scene, with a skier and criss-crossing ski-tracks in the foreground. Over this area Mathias had made a sketch in biro of a building-sculpture, so that the figure of the skier was only barely visible underneath the drawing. It was an example of the sort of thing he has done for over two decades now, under the name of "emotional architecture". I have it with me still.

solar radiation, wind, rain, gravity
stains on the mirror that can't be removed
pink blossoms down one street
asymmetrical
dust & dirt on the carpet & the furniture
car suddenly pulling up then moving on again
very irregular in time (apart from gravity)
a pile of clothes on the chair
rows of white tenements
any idealistic or imposed geometric form
the chair partly broken
yellow blossoms on the avenue
pure Platonic forms into the house
yellow mark along the base of the white wall
sound of drilling
such obvious contradiction to the forces & influences evident
stains on the ceiling
children in the playground
from molecular or astronomic contexts
paint flaking off
smoke through the air
such help is always most difficult & always falls short
of the heart's desire
beyond reasoning
inexpressible, undefinable, & inconceivable
the more we transgress
the more let us trust
the state in which there is no self-contrivance
there is no reasoning
profoundly grateful
trees & sky & stars

reflection
blue fabric
white
gleam on the back
folds
at a
pile of books
the square
the line
where the
edge
shirts on the door
postcards on
flat & round
rises
leg of the
edge
folds
light blue
yellow with floral
of the view
draped
two buttons
folded
brown
wooden cross-piece
light on the curve
white on one
two stacks
diaphanous
white
edge
set in the
cutting
shadow
at a point
bordered
blue carpet
pile of

leg curving up
red material
paper
shadow
coat on the blue
at that
white button
& folds
curved & brown
white door in
mark across
light
centre-piece
window
flaked off
rises
shadow
straight line
cord
under
where it
shadow of
& shadow
piled up
fire
edge
white paper
cord
the table-top
folded
straight line
surface
on the
wall
glaze
at

cold	park	hill	horizon	seat	mist
glass	sloping metal frame		verandahs	three locations	
sunlight	throne	horizon	hill	field	sun

Apropos of the symbolism
set within the heart
in the radiant heart
black marble
this resemblance
is too striking
repeated three times
at the centre of all being
the innermost point
a very strict relation
significance of the name
"God in us"
the seed contained in
the heart
the symbolism of the heart
the name of "seed"
the idea of the seed
in the heart must claim
our attention
different places
deep significance
to truly grasp this relation
which gives to the heart
as the centre of being
the name of Divine City
dwells at the centre of
being
"The Ether
in the heart"
realises the expanse
by its radiance within
"making of the void
something"
a concentration
this luminous expansion
it remains within the heart
a particular being
human being
by virtue

a transposition
from one of the other
which dwells in the heart
smaller than a grain
of rice
which dwells
in the heart
than all the worlds
put together
lodge in the branches thereof
dwells in the heart
not with observation
is within you
total
in all beings
neither differential nor limited
exercised from within
not at all apparent
to the eyes
from within to
without
its point of departure
with what is innermost
by relation to the ensemble
or by relation
to each of them taken particularly
"the least of all seeds"
descending / ascending
is habitually related
to the heart
what are these two ways?

Areas

For Kerry

"The Kami (gods) have no form but only function. On the contrary man has both form and action. The Gods cannot surpass the actions which have form and man cannot surpass the wonderful actions which have no form."

1.

for the dead
we sit a long time, an hour maybe
in silence

shaking with fear
I sit with her in this cold place
for something like an hour

she'll leave me to it
for hexagrams of dark water
vague smell of incense

procession of candles in the dark
candles moving in the dark
in file

or the little girl in a bridesmaid's
dress, walking on the pavement
stopping, turning, laughing

these still haunt us
spook waters
in alcoves

from the water
up, laughing /-
gasping
at you

a desire to wash the whole face
skin of the face
in the water of those basins in the
alcoves

cold of the night, I am shivering /
the smell of self-destruction

These people
later
seated in a circle
some form of
survival:

alternation of silence and
"twitterings" the girl said in an attempt at
description

an hour's lapse, we say
walked by the sea in the afternoon while he
slept

slept

and the story begins to tell us what we knew, that this
is not the whole of it

The whole of time:
as time, not
as a history – to wake in
the night

body warm from sleep,
the stairs, to wake
immersed

half-way to wake
into / out-of
time /
water /
sleep

A pressure in one part
of the self
or several

The big wind outside

Noise of the wind outside

To wake
obsessed, falling
into and out of
several dreams at once

holding onto the small objects of the room
for whatever focus can be achieved:
small yellow cloth, rectangular;
cup;
typewriter

If I love you
I send out axe-blows of music
to break the stones of the streets
I send out love to detect
bombs in the streets you tread

it is in heart only as once
they are broken *(interrupted)*
often enough: the night, the dreams
they will be continuous again

splinters of duration
something in each
splinter

crystal
shattered cube of glass

Cymbal crash or "ting" creates
the gigantic surface
stillness, silence
the door opens, closes again:
a room

brilliant ghosts
and solid,
space a wash of space

light and sound
phenomena
these enter
like entering a room

the structures now are
spoken
someone speaks
them –

he is so near
he has become indistinct
the nearer he is
the more indistinct
a woman
is in the background she is
clear to the sight

when you look back at the
passage
the space looks back at you
the way you came
the heart

the indecent light

Seated in a circle we discuss
which one should write the poem about drowning
and stay on the bank, which one
should drown:

four Irish priests, all having
lived in the Philippines
all dressed in black
all decidedly
MASCULINE:

one Irish nun who has also
lived in the Philippines:

one Filipino woman
who tells me I remind her of her son
light in the wood, light in some
unexpected space, a darkened room
the map of the world flopping all over the
floor like some absurd sheet of rubber or
an injured beast

The blonde woman
is thoughtful
in that background, she
is in the kitchen
In the foreground
the man grows blurred and
thoughtful

At this point there should occur
recollections of some slides of
the Philippines
except that I didn't bother turning up
that night
for the showing

Piano-sounds in my mind
the small mythologies, warm-blooded /
trees' shadows long on the grass, the small
animals loose in Powis Square Gardens
a place eaten by moths

And when the animals betray us?   dogs
snapping at me in the streets

2.

laughs at
the loop of story-line I saw as I strolled
one day in Epping Forest
she announced that she
was sick of "grown-up's games" –

drew a circle in green chalk on the floor
stepped inside it and disappeared

slow eyes
creature of Dostoevsky
to take in the
random violence of the streets

Drift of poems, river of
poetry

The journey is straightforward, perhaps
yet the ungathered energies are correlate
with the warp in the plan, the eccentric
space of wherever we go,
over a hill or into some chasm and out
again, mindlessly, endlessly, in love and reeling
how slow, a drift of particles

If we began to talk in the late afternoon, I said once, and
continued in this room until late in the evening
and didn't bother about the lights, we'd be
gradually subsumed

She took to skipping rope in the living-room,
leaving half-sucked lollipops on the chairs
Getting angry with her would only
make her hysterical

Grooves of the
evening, the bus-stop,
the groves, the…

a place of parks and gardens
"not even on the map"; slums and brothels
near the station
houses of the middle-class not far
heavy snow of last February

the inexorable laws of melodrama
She turned with relief in her eyes
the thrust of voices behind us
in that distance

the sky that I don't want
to people with ghosts or to close off
as some sort of erotic / magical field
of interconnections
dependencies and trysts
the body thrown forward a moment
each moment of our lives churned out
programmed by grinding fictions

in these dull, perfect networks
the figures move:
perfect, demented

scenarios such as this woman would
spin out:
bugged telephones, the expectation
of police at the door

for months I've been living this out
the sea   the mouth, which speaks
out into the core, the space
centre of sleep

the arcs
areas, demarcations

those photographs

3.

"…pre-established forms, crystallized
by law, are repugnant"

The tableware shines, the fractions of
the air, but very possibly dead

aged 79 in February 1921
Our lives have a commitment to the possibility
that freedom may prevail: the black flag
the streets lined with believers in this much
this much for five miles, in Russia, in 1921

Insomnia: which faces breathe, their
lineaments, in the
dark-
ness?

the hills gleam, a
totality
the moon bounces kinetically

windows: each four squares of
glass, sometimes different glass /

held violin-note
sound of the bow on the strings
the note held, held

not like having it rest in your
hands but it is outside
something uncontained by the atmosphere,
the wind
critical faculties at work on how to get
by without adequate shoes, coat, pants
– they don't come up with much

Roundness, shapeliness
of the hills, yet
the outline taut /
the electric violin

first Ceylon tea then sherry,
thoughts of the weather, the
nature of love
(girls)   (a girl)

they pointed out to me the terraces
below, and the trees names of the trees
picked up a leaf that too
O so pedantic

the taxis in black streets so long ago,
years ago
abstract lightning, shape of lightning
electric violin

the poem could be endless
in a park in a poor area in a wood

Gnats in the air
stories
he looks up at them, points
the country path
his face outlined with soft yellow
hair
wonder in his features

and it's Christmas, running
madly through the streets, mouth
open and hair flying, arms
akimbo
a character out of *Alice*

honey and dew-drops, a sharp
wind in a dark country lane

dispossessed as always
and without funds
or as the evening comes, a Black man
embraces me in the street
gives me 30 pence / a young girl
comes by the house, she
demands toys and won't leave
without them:

demands to look in the cellar,
searches the rooms,
the sea (the Dodecanese islands)

Moon explodes our sense of
the hills, the straight lines
of the house

the spaces are exploded /
"…harmony in an ever-changing and
fugitive equilibrium between a multitude of
varied forces and influences"

We raise a glass to our enemies
dark beer in a lighted room
in negative / tree
outside with its precise red
leaves
a fine gentle rain

We drink beer or sherry or wine
at 200 consecutive tables
from now until
half a year away: red light dominant
impinging on this scene any
scene
       broken water flashing slowly over
stones

In honour of friends
a little beer; rain on the
dark windows, a few lights outside,
blurred
part of the shared past

You and I
we love each other, we are friends:
anarkia (non-rule)

       we develop
       the surface of the laughing
       animal: poetry;
       he has the beautiful

       eyes of the gentle
       tremendous animal

       he is violent towards those who seek or protect RULE,
       the marvellous
       beast

4.

They come in out of the night, curving shining Perspex of the revolving door – the influx / outflux, revolving, shining: I wait for him for his face and body to appear in this same way

inadvertently spitting in my face wiping the last bit from her lips blocking the next, she told me she'd been considered too sentimental to become a social worker, she was drunk she told me her husband and brother (both present both drunk) didn't understand, that there was this something in her life, pressing from within, it was sentimental

not like the old woman who stood in the street and asked passers-by if they'd marry her, she must have been 70 years old and I was 21: I said no

Anecdotal nebulae: the units or sections burning outside in Powis Square Gardens; a mixed group of people stand around and burn whatever it is they burn: and they make noise, with some musicians standing there and playing wild loose jazz on trumpet saxophone and percussion the music continuing late, late and without sign of exhaustion, building in this squalid area a column, a tower, while the cops

                              stand around and watch

A Song, for Plumage
(to Steve Lacy)

1.

alternating black & white sectors
sound into light
the musician & poet prized so
low he is buried upright,
in a hollow tree trunk

snap
shots
curve, linked, in a form
I know nothing about

notes picked
from the horizontal & vertical
axes;

plucked

these images that I will never hang in the
empty house

snap
shut
they explode gently at a vantage point
for the eyes to pop open

in a house
for love
for the solid
objects

lashes of the eyes,
the way clothes fit to
the body
details of a house fit
for the descriptions & embodiments

a house which is her house
for she
accomplishes it

& waking at any moment
to see her mouth & cheeks

day/night
various forms of
opening & closing
to mirror the immense blue sea

2.

blood in the throat

a buzzing at the lips
eyes closed,   *lids*
of the camel's eyes
"the flame in the
mouth"
eyes wide open in
the lids
the flame the

form which cannot be spoken of
verging on the ridiculous
entering a room with that walk

the splendour

or: they wish to mutilate us

perched on the tree of possession

3.

this hour
laughable or *weird*
abrasions in the sky
sunset behind sheets of rough glass

as contrast
snap
I see you, instant,
wild blue

piercing monotony
an event
a thunderstorm
a flame
to light faces

against the blind
snow-dazzle
of western civilization

there is the need
to break old forms
like breaking bread

hoopla   coming into the
room or appearing from a subway
when I need to see you

variable
indeterminate
pacings
over basalt
& some other kind of stone

the air
sweat dripping down & off
a parabola

of intensity / emotion
such as: flight
such as: song

4.

across formations
a flight of birds

& each sound a
living organism,

penetration,

event

across formations

at a precise date

"love's voyage" pasted
into such areas as: bowed cymbals

stroke of the drum

between two long pieces of music
full of energy
& textural display

one minute five seconds
that
quietude of her voice:

there are times
when even an obituary note
is beautiful

the voice of it
straight melody

5.

eyes closed & head tossed back
the mouth moving, breath &
utterance, bread soaked in a thick stream,

spine,
burred glittering,   glistening

the historians move in for the kill,
their words legal tender – anal –

shouts, murmurs, whispers, the
voice
cracked, slurred

a moving network of relations,
for it to *work*
a singular intensity & mindfulness

the ways broken, obscured –
on the thrones, in the light
where they do not belong, the bloodsuckers sit
sipping blood through straws –
worked, opened up
to be

6.

deep in wet fresh grass,
the wheel   of little lights & very precise dates,
angled / disrupted
            slopes up

7.

significance of ceramic
flute
or soprano sax

all those sibilants

breath
& the thrushes & nightingales
that may accompany you

with kites and painted signs

with the single rain-drop
falling so slowly
it takes all day to fall

cigarette smoke &
cigarette ash
the single rain-drop falling
towards night,
the diamond,
the Maya with their beautiful faces
& their civilization turned to ashes in the hand

9.

shy by instinct
is that material at your wrists
hessian or silk?
it is
survival
laughter
for the frozen gesture
manipulated language your laughter strikes
across/
the room

sitting in the corner, who
is
she
&
why
birds breaking
from mouth & wrists,
"love's voyage"
to be
sung

1.

the eye sees
out of the skull
made plastic
    which I try – we try – each
to make bone again

loving her, loving him
in darkness, wishing at a crossroads
on a jewel held in the hand
of another
    other
by bus-stop, in rain and lamp-light

tears
    (tears)
in dream before knowledge

walked
under the pink and white blossoms
blossoms on branches
at night
walked under and back again
on the street

after-image
or recurrence:
striped curtain, light
in the window – suddenly
goes to black

elsewhere: appearance of a girl
slowly skipping rope
young girl's grace
outside my door
elsewhere: appearance of a girl, younger
girl, around a corner
on the island of Patmos

suddenness
           of her appearance
elsewhere: child I told my name
last day I worked in a showroom
sweeping and polishing
joined with her
in a game of hide-and-seek

2.

went into a shop
in the next street
bought a glass object
egg-shaped
to fit
the hand

in the street itself
a house
one house
and not another
        a cat
large, white
outside on the steps
asleep in the sun

unreal the cat lies
in another space

opposite: raises its head
to watch itself
            figure
of remembrance
there and not there
                palpable
unbelief

3.

I had gone into town to meet my friend Michael, to drink coffee at the little West End cafés he likes so much, and talk. As we walked down a street towards an underground station, I noticed in front of us a girl I thought I recognised – she looked back & then I felt sure of recognition, as she must have, because she began to run.

Dark intersection where one year two years are meshed with this present, in dream, unearthly crossroads. How the night eats through wood & flesh. Heart's *anarkia* which has been brought to *what* division & loss?

The Master of Hearts, that figure of authority, offers black & sticky sweets. He instructs his followers to freeze their whirling bodies in ridiculous postures at his command. And they love him.

Stone steps in light – a large white cat asleep in the warmth. In dream the girl came to ask, shyly, if she could see me, to talk. And that, after so very long a time, was forgiveness.

1.

Someone comes, out of the distance
form & face
     clearing
. . . .
That night the town area near the sea.
Dreamt of a girl child; her life thrown
amongst brutal, absurd people
in a house of ignorance
the cobbled streets, narrow lanes of memory.

2.

Descending –
the head framed
by rectangle reflected silver

in the large high window
(opaque glass of door
lit from behind)

& 'the head' frontal – a
face – mine.

3.

A form falling
&
the form of falling –

white sail
in darkness.
. . . .
Beatrice – *Beata
Beatrix*, Rossetti's painting
in reproduction

on my wall, while
I slept, detached itself
by its weight

the sound waking me from a dream
white shape falling across
me cutting into the dream.

Conscious of it, still screaming out, conscious
of a figure sitting up in bed in
dark screaming out.

4.

Lit windows
in a dark frame –

various
boxes of night.
. . . .
Love returns
where I

turn upon word
of night;

dark edge of
building, white wood,
lighted
room.

The blinding moment
capitulates;

to retention of a schema
invisible because inside
the eye.

Glass shatters, bursting outwards:
Look, she said, *it's snow*
so the parents hold her up to view it

in another time, where the
movement of those particles
is slow as the most dream-like *adagio*.

Or, inside the lift we wonder
where we are. A

street. A gravel path. A pond
& trees. Pain reddens
these, reflection of blood,

but what is incalculable
the moon illumines.

Screens. Through which
body breathes across to body,
slender reflections off walls,
tender darknesses.

Three Poems for Julius Bissier

1.

What has happened
to the shattered image
of the face?

 – A dream answers,
in endurance –
of the Milky Way's hazy glow

spread through the rooms
of a house. It makes its way
along the spine –

in attending to these rooms
for the first time, (cloud & light),
I will remember them

for my life. It issues & endures
with the ink forming on paper
images of generation

& regeneration; unity
of male & female; personal tribute
on the death of a friend.

2.

A river flowing through
window, street, early light.

(Argument continued
down passageways:
inaudible.)

Funerary
inscriptions,
archaic –

two cords,
the sexes.

3.

Dark hanging lamp –
dunkle Ampel –
in this window
& the dark blue sky:
weightless,
beyond pain;
this golden light.

Portals

– Any such
thing, you say:
doorway, cup,
mouth or hand,
legend congeals there.
– Can't get over it: I've
lost to compassion,
luminous dark point
against which flail
the night's
white shreds, flick-
erings, drum raps.

•

Recumbent –
hand beside head.
Fire over stone,
bells in wind.

The image: *parinirvana*;
caught by the eye
as the bus moves on.

Later: traffic
streaming past,
I sat a long time
in peace.

•

Arch through arch. A face in stone looks in the direction of each cardinal point upon itself, dreams across the ruins, black and white points, patches and splashes of stone, vegetation, ground and sky.

Seated bronze figure, arm off, impossible scale. Behind its profile: the sky, white.

•

A house for blessing the dead, stone dragons guarding past long grass and broken fence: recurring at intervals through childhood into manhood. I stood on the steps, for the photograph; then walked with mother and sister up the street towards a high roof, sun on sheets of new tin. Crowd, wharf and ocean, as extension.

•

I sat listening to a very long piece of music for piano, sustained in its intense quietude and its articulation of a formal architecture intersecting with randomized accumulations of sounds. (– Alpine bells in wind. As we sat together drinking tea, we discussed his work. – Some of my music, he said, is written with the notes falling 'as quick as lightning'. *But the other pieces* – I follow a strict program for discovering just how slowly I can pace each sound in relation to its neighbouring sound. My music, he continued, provides a means – for the contemplation of the way order and chance interrelate in our lives. It is a symbolic interpretation of that interrelationship. My conventions provide me with a way of achieving this with – perhaps I can say – unselfconsciousness.) After a while I became aware of a woman and her child in the front row; the little girl, a blonde-haired child with star-shaped ornaments in her hair and a face expressive of the most fetching sobriety, could bear the long duration of this slow, quiet, uneventful music only by attending to her mother's face, holding her hand, and eventually cradling her head first on the woman's shoulder, then on her lap.

•

> Fayum. Only the eyes
> speak, a window
> lets us in
> on no other thing. Death

eats all it may. We
have words to bear,
stories that will be told.

.

Music, he said, gives
the right analogy; modes
of expression

analyzed out
into permutations
of features.

The face, I said, effaces
the orders, greater than addition
in the life of imagination.

.

Perpetuum mobile –
mechanical dream –
violin bowed and plucked
in frantic whimsicality:
token, stain on the air.

.

The hands of the huge bronze statue showed reassurance and bestowal. It was raining out there in the garden, a light delicate rain. I had gone there many times when visiting my friend, and I was there again when I couldn't visit him, as he had died several months before. I wandered through its spaces, looking once more at the flowers, the Japanese stone lanterns and the temple bells which rested on the ground; and at the small fountain and the Chinese bronze flower-vessel with a sculptured dragon writhing around its tall rounded form, the dragon's mouth extended wide.

.

Rain upon black branches. At the door: a woman in a red gown, a child before her on the steps. Diadem. Eyes of the mind. – Yellow leaves falling through the darkening air, falling and falling.

•

We looked out from the portals of the old church – out across the city. Bright, spectral blue lights in the square. Groups of people sitting on the blue steps around the fountain, drinking wine. Yet, it was – quiet. He spoke of his admiration for the Siennese masters – Duccio and Simone Martini – and of his life-long attempt to find that same luminosity of colour for himself. – Sitting in his studio, I looked at the painting of the Angel of Annunciation, tall robed figure with his head bowed slightly, and a forearm raised, with fingers extended in the making of a sign. The Virgin was outside the space of the painting, the Angel standing at the extreme right, facing out of the edge of the picture. Behind him, in warm, sonorous colours, fruit and a glass stood on a table; behind them, a window looked out onto a serene landscape of hills and trees.

Cells

Where movement's arrested, an apparition is loosed upon discomforted senses. (I look closer, then closer again, magnifying, brooding.) Snow-visage; snow-hand, reaching out.

°

(Niobe) wept herself to stone.

°

In a photograph – *dark stain* – of a group of strangers, I am struck and held by one face: a resemblance that leaves me stricken.

This young girl (posed with her schoolfellows) fuses with another person, so that I can now see that other as she must have been, years before I first met her.

°

The narrow streets of deep-rutted paving stones, with fountains at the intersections, lead me to this small garden, where she stands, still and solitary. In the night.

°

A contrast of purple flowers and deep green foliage, in sharp light, had drawn my eye. Walking back the same way, night had negated it

– permitting a ghostly after-image to remain. The time between: an interregnum.

.

Moved: grasped: shaken: struck: taken up: taken over: flooded: broken apart.

.

Memory: stand again
at her window and see
a sparrow

searching the ground.
Reverse
the positions: I look in

on a bird perched
amongst decanters,
dishes with pabulum,

everything soaked
in the colours
of an opaque

privacy.
Pompeian
interior. O

where else
to be buried
in ash.

Aura

He was unconscious when they pulled him from the car's wreckage; weeks then went by, with his mother keeping a vigil each day in the hospital.

It was so long a time to be perfectly enclosed within helplessness. But I wake thinking of the body wasted to a skeleton, the wet earth in a hand's grasp before release; and the circle's shaken into flames.

.

The surface of the table, black in darkness, retains deep in its fibres gleams of earring and necklace.

.

Walking in the British Museum, we passed a number of Fayum portraits. She commented that she had made pencil studies of these pictures of the dead from Roman Egypt – which I find more moving than almost all other human images. Later, seated in a café, she asked: Shall I draw your portrait? – No, I replied; I'd rather you didn't.

.

The colours, mixed with the heated beeswax, form a likeness. Greek lettering, white, spells a name, and the word "farewell".

Those eyes given definition by death look on as if no death could end their seeing.

.

Enduring as faith not as evidence: a fan of yellow, green and blue light framing a head against a white wall.

.

Should I say, *I knew you by your gaze* – I would mean that what endures is the way you arrest and sustain whatever's gathered in your vision. But there is one whose gaze shocks me, and draws love.

A face that reveals more than I'm accustomed to in a person's features. And not in any simple sense; for I cannot say what exactly is being revealed. I am taken into it as if moving along a dizzying projection that I sense as endless.

And if compassion is a visible part of it, so too is pain.

.

Striae, that cut an ambience.

The unspoken penetrates into the table where we sit, in a lambent space where what's loved in the human gaze is irreducible, intractable.

.

In conversation I'd made use of the term *personhood*, culled from the writings of the theologian Heinrich Ott on the spiritual dimensions of personal being. Someone commented, with good-natured mockery, that she liked the term because it made her think of a little man with an umbrella over him.

.

Quavering in the air or the mind: voice composing flame. Cantillation.

He turned at the door. Emptied out his case: the dark green sleeping bag, pullovers, socks, the small pile of jazz records. I saw him, by underground and bus, to the airport, and we parted. As I turned to go back the same way, I realized he was dead.

.

I wake in the dark, amongst the surfaces of things; with the gaze of human eyes impressed through layers of forgetfulness.

Threshold

– If I died, and then reappeared, would you believe it was me? she asked.

– How could that happen? I replied.

– If my body was recreated, and I appeared here again, would you see it was me?

– Could that happen? I asked, turning towards the window, and realizing as I did that it was pouring down outside, yet the sound of the rain against the windowpanes and down in the street had until then made no entry into my consciousness.

.

A kinetically whitened field of vision, street – hail on road and footpath, car-roofs and house-roofs. A doorway sheltered us.

A threshold beckoned to us.

.

    – To sit quite still
    in the movement first into the dark,
    then intense light:
    eyes fixed ahead; long
    straight hair, pulled back
    off the forehead
    of the girl's face.

    Stopped and drawn forth.

.

And the *soma pneumatikon* would have eyes that would not be yours – and yet be yours; just as the eyes that would recognize them would no longer be identical to those you knew on streets and in rooms and cafés, and yet you would know them as the same.

The Image

A painter once spoke of how he had tried many times to make an image of the human scream, cry of terror, pain, horror. – And I have always wished, he said, to paint, also, the human smile. It was a wish that remained apart from any known attempt; let alone realization.

.

I imagine you standing on worn steps of stone, with your thin, child's legs; your eager smile; and gaze that gives back the ineluctable. And the image is terrible to love's eyes – all ruin is spelt to these eyes; each moment, the ruin faced.

.

Streetlamps at the margins, through the central field of obscurity you would move, into the dark. In my room, a lamp's thrust of illumination deforms the outline of its globe. I scrape or rub at the image before me, bringing gray, silver or white from blackness.

Bagatelles

(for Howard Gold)

I picked up the book; on its cover, there were characters in black ink over a gray wash, which I couldn't read. I put it down again and walked along the narrow dark passage until I came out into the blinding rain. – One evening we had been walking together by a canal near where my friend at that time lived, and I found myself thinking of the following fable: In the beginning, the gods placed in a circumscribed area all those spirits who wished to do nothing but continue deceiving each other, hurting each other, acting out all the petty spectacles of egoism which had sustained their interest during their lives on earth: this was hell. But the almost unlimited possibilities of inflicting injury on each other – in the absence of mortality – led the spirits to perform the most gross indignities and savageries upon their fellows and, in their rage for cruelty, themselves. Hell degenerated into a place of perpetual torment and madness, in which its denizens took turns at the roles of dominator and dominated, possessor and possessed, torturer and tortured.

•

So much have I spoken
of you, walked so much,
devoting myself
to your shadow,
that you have gone.
And after everything,
perhaps there remains for me
to be only a shadow
among shadows;
less real
than the shadow that moves
with joy
over the sundial of your days.

(– Voice: which travels along a deathly route, through *the hecatombs of the concentration camps*, ways of manifest evil; bringing words beyond death.)

•

In dream the figure turned, ran back into the burning house, the sound abruptly cut. – She drank too much, the psychiatrist had said, she was sexually unstable, and she was suicidal; and *this* pathological woman was the most important person in his life. (Saying it in contempt.) – Why shouldn't she have been? I'd replied mildly. And dreamed: felt terror, as I accompanied a huge brown rabbit who stood upright, clothed to the neck with a body-length brown garment. His name was Hunter Rabbit. He kept on shooting people down as we passed them on our way (why was I with him?), taking a snub-nosed gun from a pocket in his clothing. – *Why are you doing this, for God's sake?* I said. – Nuts, he said; those guys had it coming. Back at my place, I took down a book on the painter Bosch, to check out a suspicion that I harboured, while Hunter Rabbit drank his whisky-sour. Sure enough, there he was, except that in the painting he carried a pole from which a naked human body hung suspended by the ankles. – Sure, he said, looking over my shoulder, Jerry the Painter; yeah, I knew Jerry the Painter.

•

The motorcycle skidded and went over on the dark rainy street, with the rider's leg caught under it. She lay there, her body arched and helpless with shock or pain. – Bombs rip up the streets, rip cars apart and the bodies of people within those cars and on the pavement and road. She tells me this, and the streets and the night take on strange colours, those of another city, another country, fluorescent reds, blues, yellows and greens blurred in the reflection of wet streets, and washed-out pastel colours. A chorus crosses the water: threnody.

Appearance & Event: 16 Poems

"Though every effort will be made to give experience and thought as directly as possible, and as nearly as may be toward their full detail and complexity…, the job is chiefly a sceptical study of the nature of reality and of the false nature of re-creation and of communication."
James Agee

"When you play with authority, then that's what the music is about, like oooooh baby, and sing it."
Cecil Taylor

the length is as large as the breadth
(neutral, shapeless)

so we measured the wall
according to the measure of a man, that is, of the angel
(not large, not small,   sizeless)

and I saw no temple therein
(no unconsciousness)

what size   is a man?

if you cut the painting, the man
bleeds   at that point
where he became man

          Ad Reinhardt,
his shadow   against the wall
a shadow   of his figure   which is   absent

what size is a man?
being dead
     where the city lies
(formless) (lightless) (colourless)
the wall (trisected)
as wide as a man's outstretched arms
Ad Reinhardt,   & what is unconsciousness   or no
                              unconsciousness?

there is fire on the water,   fire
in the air.
your eyes –
opposite, in clarity.
where you or I disappear
flowers burn up in the absence.

Penetration: one
image & another.

Her position in the air:
over me.

(Her hair
hanging down, one word more
to describe it.

& her eyes & lips. One
word more
& the words break / split:)

I saw her again,
April 21 1976
in the heat & light of the
instant

"plain as day"
before it wasn't her.

The invisible form
oscillates through the visible,
brief, quick, insistent....

Someone will stand on the pavement
in possession
& this is so near the truth,
it is the cutting-edge of misery.

On the pavement, on the
pavement there is an outline
which grows

& comes again to nothing
out of the eye,
or an irregular stain.

When I worked at a bookshop
across from the university,
a girl leapt from the Engineering Block
onto the street below –

the one thousandth which is not emptiness –
what is that?

…external kisses have been made
the fiery chariot   to mount me
into the bosom
of the King of Glory,   said
Abiezer Coppe (1649)   of
the drinking, smoking, swearing
Ranters –

he was riding a horse,
lost in a forest, & he came upon a stranger;
he spoke, narrated, &
gave to the man.

The excitement in the speech unfolds
how the mouth draws honey, dirt,
a question   of desire. This
established, the information burns,
not merely flows, it burns.

Burning the house down was so that the wife could have a house in heaven.

A climactic scene: I am executed by a Nazi firing squad.

...when the atomic bomb was dropped, he was frightfully burned, as shown by the postcards of his back which he used to sell, autographed. He left the city, after being "over-active in anti-war protests".

They do not move persistently in one direction; they do not follow leaders; they do not plunge recklessly into the sea and commit suicide.

I have polished brass door-handles & door-plates;
I have cleaned toilets & sorted through trash;
I've carried around other people's correspondence in sacks;
I've stamped & shelved books in libraries;
I've worked with figures & done filing.

These are only some of the jobs I've had to do.

I am footloose & shiftless.

Rich people are abounding in resources, productions, etc.;
they are fertile & well-filled;
they are precious, costly; high-flavoured & fat.
They will not come out & play.

When you get bitten in the neck it leaves a small wound
instantly recognisable. It's OK. They're beautiful, you're beautiful.

Silver lines etched into the night bind us
to the window, a boat moves slowly on the water.
We gaze out; other eyes gaze back into ours.
It is the violence that lacerates
all feeling & all delusion, to move beyond the window
& that window; blood soaks into the carpet
under bare feet. What sea
have we come to, it strikes
the smallest thing: *the radiant heart.*

In the night all the given names cut through
me. The child who has dreamt   pathetically
of the *aristocratic* & the *noble*, her image is in the snow,
she pushes the corners of her mouth into a smile.
Walking   at the edges   of sleep,
how her image is in the snow;
how a room is erased; & the street covered
by the falling snow & we
walk faster.

for George Alexander,
in the memory of that colour
even if the word is the "same"
it is the colour said contrary to the colour
of what we have been taught, the visible world,
– burning against the pavement we walk,
– pulling sharp against & through
what we have been taught, each thing is, into
the motional knowledge of a thing as it is.

Our words are a violence, George
both
moving through & against the snow
of "our" language (our birth).
Artisan's fire.
The hour is baked, to be eaten
in the care of the heart's blood,
as trust is, I cannot separate.

The narrative is broken by
successive flashes, lightning &
rain-bursts in the mind
& in the nerves.   What
does it matter whose mind it is,
Berkman's, Pasternak's,   mine
or yours. It matters, like a
hypothesis matters: the narrative endures.
& maybe there's more drama to it. The telephone
rings. Someone   walks in. Turns
to exit. A sudden phrase by which we know.

The narrative   is established
by successive flashes, interruptive
cohesion. The sexuality of its endurance:
he stares, she looks, she goes away
& he stares. A man broke down. A boy
broke down. & all the time something is building
inside a voice, where the whole   thing matters
like hell, the endurance, the transmission:

Berkman tells how when Emma   Goldman
was first allowed to visit him
in the prison, he couldn't
talk, couldn't   keep his eyes away
from the trinket around her neck.
Years later she narrated the same story,
it was   another part of the centre,
the sentences unfolding a wilderness   not his.

There is a confusion of voices   & the voices
exist within a confusion: a sea-
drift of words
in public. Time   of the crossing.

Two halves never fit together. The polarities
keep everything in motion, they are
the order. Two halves   never make a whole.
As Wittgenstein once told Russell, any statement
including *the world* is nonsense. The boat
sets off.

The polarities call us   into service
of *the stars and wine,* where *the song-cry* is.
But where we are, the sea carries our time.

Or a meadow under water. The public words
given each other in private, cover a void
treacherously. Even
our materiality is an endurance: void
shot through with brilliant splinters of duration,
points of crystal & ruby.
                    Dark, I wrote,
                    to the market.

If the images of friends have returned,
returned, in public places, where & when
they were not,   could I call this
a superimposition   of two systems, two
material planes?   Is it confusion,
or some sort of clarity?   – Certainly
there was, in each case, light   attendant....

This ghostliness may, in fact, be the very
stuff of form – the *light waves travel
through completely empty space.*   You
make an appearance or   I appear:
like a superimposition
of single images,
the shapes pile up   in a structure;

but instead, the movement is like a signal-beam
travelling the length
& the attraction grows.

Wind – or the fiery mind.

Children's faces are caught by the eye
as they run past,   as light
is held by the sharp leaves   of the holly,
a surface of light.   I have used the word *love*
seldom enough, for it to be enough.

She turns everything into wine, the man said;
rose-petals, apples, plums, – you name it.

The Blessing or Spiritual Influence
compared to wine.

The signal *transferred as an invisible stream
along the length,* the entire length…
compared to wine?

Liz said that at the showing
we'd be treated to wine.

Held by the image I am caught
yet I   caught my own voice
moving,   coming out by a different route.

Quieter, as it is tonight (or in late
afternoon)   desire moves
me to the outermost edge.

The dark warm water.

An ambulance
wet streets
cars
a man on a stretcher –

Gaudí the architect was knocked   down
by a streetcar, she said;

she stood, Frances, at the window with the others;
I stood   at the other window.

This rain is added to Gaudí's accident
& death.

The names: Palacio Güell,
Sagrada Familia, Casa Milá....
Am I to demean that eccentric
grandeur, that the names
are not ours, do not,
have not
sheltered us.... (*I
am middle-class*, she said; *aren't
we all middle-class?*)

Taken to the poor people's hospital by accident,
poor Gaudí.

This rain is –
the human misery is –
added unto his death,

poor Gaudí.

Poem for Emmy Hennings

She died in great poverty in some village,
Emmy Hennings, & I can't remember the details
of those final years or the name of the place,
the "where" which could be connected to the term "woman"
& to the concept of "soul", which is a matter
of drawing images: drawing, with a pencil
the outline of a face & a body.

Meine Mutter der Tod, (My mother is death
mein Vater das Licht. (My father is light
in the air & on the sea; I kiss my friend.
Meine Speise das Brot, (My food is bread
mein Grab ein Gedicht. (My grave a poem.
We stand simultaneously   at the end & the beginning.
Her figure wanders over some area that I cannot recognise, &
the missing connection is "sea" for which is substituted
the lakes of Switzerland where it was, I think, she died.

The Soprano

In Mittersill one night, at the end of the Second World War, Anton Webern stepped outside his son-in-law's house to smoke a cigar. An American soldier bumped into him in the dark and – thinking he was being attacked – shot Webern dead.

A friend told me of an open rehearsal of Webern's *Cantata No. 1* that she once took part in. In the second section, when the soprano began to sing Hildegard Jone's words about the maple-seed as *the bearer of new life*, a child walked across from the audience and aimed a toy pistol at the soprano's head, keeping it there until the end of her solo.

Funeral Music (for R. C. Kenedy)

I imagine the sort of funeral he'd have wanted: the coffin borne aloft by a bevy of gorillas. What sort of gorillas would carry Robert's coffin? Amiable gorillas. Or: devoted ones.

The music would be provided by the rhythmic chest-pounding of those gorillas following the coffin. They would be announcing the dimensions of a zone.

Kiss Me

– Kiss me, said the mouse; now put your ear close, I want to whisper something to you.... And the mouse whispered obscenity after obscenity.

The cat lay on the chair, just below the windowsill, and sang. It had its eyes closed, as if near to sleep or in a sort of ecstasy, and it was singing – but I closed my ears, and now I was screaming, it sang of such horrors....

– You must leave here, said the dog, you must leave immediately: you're in danger; come away with me. But I didn't trust the dog.

The Oak Tree in the Garden

He stood up from the table, saying: I don't ask you about fifteen days ago. But what about fifteen days hence? Then, banging on the table: Why do you not go where there is no cold and heat? Jumping up and down, then doing a cartwheel across the floor, he said: Oh, where are the rivers and mountains and the great earth? I preach what I cannot practise, and I practise what I cannot preach. When you shut the light from your eyes and become a corpse, how can you free yourself? The twenty-sixth of August, I should give you sixty blows with a stick, but today I forgive you. What were *you* doing this summer? Standing on his head, he continued: The trunk is visible in the autumn wind. A dung-wiping stick. If you have no staff, I will take it away from you. Transmitted. There are one hundred and eight beads in the daytime; at night there are one hundred and eight. The opposite of statement.

Standing on his feet again, he picked up his empty tea-cup and threw it into a corner of the café where it broke into numerous pieces, while he shouted at the same time: Three pounds of flax!

The waiter, enraged by this behaviour, caught hold of him and pushed him out of the door and onto the pavement. The oak tree in the garden, said the waiter.

.

They had been sitting in the café for five minutes or so, talking.

If you don't see a man for thirty days, he said, do not think he is the same man. How about you?

She shrugged. Hmm, change, she thought: hmm, yes: change, change.

Well, she said, of course everyone's life is subject to change.

I didn't know everyone had a life.

She smiled slightly. He said: But you – ?

My life has changed.

You cannot even enter your own bed without a burden on your mind, he said.

Shit, she thought: do I have a good one for you.

A broken mirror, he continued, never reflects again; fallen flowers never go back to the old branches. If you think you really come and go, that is your delusion. What you did was a mere shifting of the wind. In the end it would result in your downfall.

She was silent for a minute; then she said: There was my husband....

One cannot tell for sure at night. Such apparitions are best inspected in daylight.

Oh fuck, she thought. But she just looked at him, without comment.

What kind of eyes do they have who transmigrate to the six worlds? he asked; but it was not really a question.

I returned to him, she said simply.

A bee never returns to its abandoned hive.

I don't happen to be a bee, she replied.

My dear, he said, taking her hand. Cognition is a delusion and noncognition is senseless. All living objects are upside down, deceived as to their true nature and pursuing objects.

Oh *fuck,* she thought.

Why do you plant this pine tree? he enquired.

She opened her mouth as if to speak, but he stopped her by asking – or saying: And so you went back to him?

Yes. You know that.

Your thoughts and your emotions: they were like burglars sneaking into a vacant house.

Fucking hell, she thought: what did I ever see in this arsehole?

The path is like a mirror, he said. What did you wear before you were born? You should observe my body thoroughly, otherwise you will regret it later. Your selfish discrimination separates heaven and earth and turns them both into hell!

Oh, God! the woman exclaimed.

•

Or perhaps: one face saddened by knowledge – however much given in advance – and the other entirely unaware, so obsessed is he by his "awareness", cherished, hugged to himself, bought at a high price.

And so, out of anger and disillusionment, the sadness comes to birth in her look and endures.

Where are they? A distance abolishes the café-scene. Somewhere, immensely near it seems, a wind blows in the leaves of an oak tree, as a figure wanders alone in the garden at night.

Of the World. Of Power

1.

Pedestrian descriptions of landscape: little watercolour sketches. Constant pain in the head. People came to see him. He liked that.

She was attracted to water as a picturing of flux, as a dangerous and a mystical element. She would eventually drown herself – other ways had been tried. She felt she was, by means of her art, throwing herself as it were against death, in defiance. Death had a way of noticing such enthusiasms. She had become famous.

She once had an experience where she saw a church as it had existed two centuries before. Now, what is the significance of this? None.

The time-illusionism, that is, the picture of time as infinite regression, imagined in the context of a pseudo-metaphysics, is fully realised in Ouspensky's *Strange Life of Ivan Osokin*; it is viciously manipulative and not only not a key to some sort of liberation, but itself actively participative in an individual and collective spell.

Persistence of recognition: such as the way the constellations get linked with desire and with the monotonous labyrinths of city streets, streets and alleyways. She said she was good at fortune-telling, and she liked to do birth-charts for people, though she never did get around to doing mine. She always did such erratic things. I invented stories about her to make appearances add up: for example, *I see myself like a queen in a fairy-tale; I pretend to be the greatest, most famous whore in history.*

He influenced the cosmic fluid in the bodies of those who sought him out; particles of light passed from him into them. "The eyelids become moist; respiration is short and spasmodic; and the breast rises and falls tumultuously; tremors begin along with precipitate and brusque movements of the limbs or the entire body." He had a pet canary. He hypnotised the canary. He had a pet cat. He hypnotised the cat. "As soon as I pointed my wand at her left side, Mlle. Belancourt staggered and fell to the floor in violent convulsions." He told a woman to reduce her heartbeat to nothing and she obeyed him.

I'd met the woman on the platform of an Underground station; she was terrified of some drunks who were being rowdy, and she insisted that there was a man following her. We got off the train at the same stop; then she was afraid of walking home by herself (it being past midnight), so I offered to accompany her. She invited me in, but her intentions seemed extremely confused; she alternated between paying me compliments and stressing her moral purity. I left about two in the morning without much having happened. She insisted that I give her my address and that I take hers. I don't expect to see her again. It's somehow occurred to me that that might be the only interpersonal encounter in some person's entire life.

2.

I remembered myself.
Elements of the landscape, such as foliage, loom largely out of scale.
I forgot to remember myself!
It was a good representation of myself, or at least: fair. I am several. My footprints, in the snow or in the sand, are all over the place.

She said that since she'd been practising self-remembrance, she'd made great progress: she was able to wash the dishes now.

Objective music is conscious music, something that can be directed. I have achieved the power and the control. Whatever is objective can kill a person. Objective music, he said sipping his Russian tea, can kill a person.

The structure involves repetition which is interesting in itself as well as being a pain in the arse.

"I have been here before" or "It's all happening again" or "The same fucking thing!" Which is nonsense. There is nowhere in the past or future to place the feet, and the present is elsewhere, the feet step into a burning river, you said. – I could relate much more to that.

She left the restaurant without me. This, I sighed, *is* a structural repeat.

He sold carpets as a ruse, also as a living. He had theories about *the decorative*, like all such people.
She was keen on the decorative too. She was choosy about clothes; she liked bad prints, mild pop music, and novels. The other woman wrote novels and poems descriptive of a sort of languid suffering. Or maybe

they were *prescriptive* of a languid suffering. She believed in socialism and seemed to be practising to be an aristocrat. At any rate, she eventually became a Catholic.

The blood gushed through the fingers held over her mouth, hot sticky ooze.

He offered them sweets, wrapped in black. The leaves of the trees were black and sticky.

I took a chance but a thunderstorm came up half-way through what I was saying. When I say "half-way" I don't mean exactly half-way, like, the centre, but it's an expression.

"Objective music can kill a person" is an expression too. So is "Everything has happened before". But they are persuasive as to a *kind* of reality. People die, over and over.

1.

a mist & a circle of light.
cars in a line, & pictures of dancers.
some figures
by imitation
other,
& a train
in which I arrive.

cars appear
stopped in a haze.
the dancers photographed
in a circle of light are thrown
by imitation beyond
imitation, the cars can know
nothing of this

at the railway-crossing. the
dancers one
person, two persons, then more:
horses, hogs, pan-lids: some
of them will kill themselves
in this imitation.

2.

angular. a person's shadow-image –
mine – folded
on lit white material
where I wash;
the image, split, continues.

3.

cars have stopped in a line
in the fog. over the golf-course

it is thick & damp
& as we walk there
my friend tells of this last
year, his wife in the hospital
as if another person
all that time. light
beckons, the only marking
over the rise.
(water in our shoes, & I cough continually.)
we come out into silence, stillness.
we continue walking on into the calm, quiet. fog
or story – I am
caught, moving
in it, for breath.

Slides

Young men and women, with dark glasses,
drinking coca-cola,
watch
the great tower, burning,
fall;

in translation, horizontal bands climb
the image. Voices
blow across
the landscape: *For God's
sake,* he shouted at her,
*for all
this time,
carrying my
words around with you? Can't you grow up?*

Fire; wind across the repetitions
of the burning structure
which falls....

.

Long black beard
and a limp – that was how
he was remembered:

blurred image – as through water – or heat-haze.
Yet *false,* rather than blurred:
memory

not being that diamond-heart,
colourless,
more true than we know.

.

Blue shadows on the steps,
lighted window – colours thrown

by the dark into relief. Acquaintance
jailed for killing his girlfriend, keeping

her severed body in a trunk; or
a friend murdered on the street: so our
images darken, in love.

– Yama: how I hate you, may you
truly come to hear the Buddha's words and
yourself be saved.

.

"Why don't you go over to Yama's place
to play?" "He's *different* – "

Yama, King of the dead, King of
Hell, whose underlings
in retribution
torture the dead –
illusionistic events
in illusionistic spaces
tenebroso.

"So if he's *not* like
the other children – does that mean
you can't *play* with him?"

.

Something stands where nothing does:
long light on a vase
blue-hued, held slide.

Who owns the image, the projection –
who owns the love it owns?

.

She was pointed out, in a café;
her little girl with arms around her and
her head on the woman's belly.

The burning structure falls through air –
autumnal leaves, blue-grey sky.

.

My sister and I walked several blocks
of our neighbourhood to view
a fine sunset. This
was years ago yet less far back
than when she chased me
smack into a sharp tin edge
and blood ran down my face.

Sister holds flowers
in her wedding picture,
her husband a stranger to me,
in front of the white and blue
stone entrance of the church.

.

Visitors have photographed
what at each time remains
in the slow demolition
of the flats opposite.

Grey-white façade,
pink smoke behind
wind-driven out,
or lifted over top
to the sky.

A fire at early morning,
nearing the end.

·

Driving into Exeter to get a train, I remembered coming to a large restaurant like this one I now saw, having just arrived in another city. John had taken me there straight from the bus, for afternoon tea. And now John almost a year dead. I remembered my first meeting with him – I'd been met at the bus-station, it was already dark, and we went first to a pub before continuing to John's place. Sitting in the pub, John said of a review I'd written of his translations, how he was amazed to see them noticed: he'd thought it would have been years before it would happen.

·

A little girl will come
to stand within the place
of entrance while we watch.

Beyond hope, in our watching
we are moved
with her
for emptiness.

We do not come into the entrance
but for emptiness
are moved to witness this girl,
how she comes to stand
within her own

mystery
past hoping.

•

Yama and Mara,
King of hell and god of evil,
went out to play together.

Profusion of buttercups
above a wall
was the first thing they saw.

Together these children
went to pick flowers
through an endless field.

Unity

1.

An acute music gathers us
to its strangeness. It goes on
& on, from an
excess of dimension.
Anagogical.

"Unity is so
strange, breaking
the familiar apart."
With this saying, we have met
in doorways & corridors; turned, laughing –
attending each other's eyes.

2.

Way, itself
cries out
from dream – dwelling there
in a transformation
of shining stones, we passed

through, it was a corridor
shifted back & forth
in articulation. – I could scarcely
tell what we were, awakening
from a story

of disguises,
to a sea
of unmixed blue.

3.

His friend's music
needed those contrasts

his paintings abandoned,
to accompany their vision….

My friend's youngest child
(she told me) turned around
as she was feeding him, placed
a piece of food
in her own mouth.

My writing must also, along
what unfamiliar way,
be company?

4.

You enter, leave, come back:
a door banging against
a field, the extent

& enclosure. A light coming on
in a room across the way, may break
the life of our eyes: and

simply that it is
a room & it is
a light, unwarranted.

The woman showed me a drawing
by one of her children: figure labelled *néant*:
they have to see

"nothing" as a person, she said. At the mercy,
by the mercy, of love –
nothing else, we come

gathered up into meeting. Brokenness
of it all: beating of wings: hands a
marvellous beating of wings.

Orientation

Saying something about death….
Rules of translation….
Grid-pattern, shadows on
the verandah –

bright lattice.

•

Car's red light passes between
a row of black trees
and grey-white building
under large white light.

I sit at the window –
one red light, another –
his voice
speaking of the paintings,
passes over the trees
and grey-white façade,
white light in dark.

•

The top-beam appears curved,
light shining on its centre –
regular partitions of the floor
brightened in the same way.

Regular white spaces,
deep recess,
framed by infinite black.

∙

Paintings uniformly dark.
Angry, mystified "viewers"
often slashed them.

(On board with the black
hangings of silk and cotton
we were enjoined to think of death.

– I put my fingers
to the black stone, and
my fingers to my lips.

So many people
around it –
I could not kiss it.)

∙

She said, There is no refuge
from beauty nor beauty's

loneliness: his work went past
what his admirers expected:

they wanted the old paintings.
God knows what

he had to go through; and what solace
in that poverty and neglect.

∙

Hot tar
in the rain.

Bitter, moving through
the mind –
voices flaring, dying –

smoke drifting in wind,
driven across water.

•

Eyes search
in all the rain
floods off
roofs, floods
the streets –

search out
any sign
to breach
finality.

His paintings
darkened,
non-objective –

and you and I
were in that
same rain.

Background Music

She showed

round face yet expressive,
smiling, showed me

the room, packing-case
slats forming exterior –
books jammed
against, achieving
in places a wall
distinct.

What,
I asked, if it should rain? The roof, she answered,
long eaves of the roof.

.

Flutter – outside.
Hands clapping.

The house. Walls.

With that noise going on
a man lies on the pavement
gasping, groping

(film).
A projection of walls.

.

Roof,
tent structure
with high points and
gentle curves.

The voice – *glissandi*,
and contrasts of register, tempo:
juxtapositions   acting in
a room set off
by colour then
another.

Achieving one
colour then
another

embodiment.

•

White-painted metal chairs
and white metal tables
in dull afternoon light.

Next door to the garden
in the white-painted room
a man leapt upon a chair
to give, impromptu, a lecture:
a dream of a chair,
dull, technical, dated –
sadly dated. We
sat outside –

talked secretively
about the androgynous-looking girl
opposite, in the floppy hat.

Inside, another man upset them, the beautiful
young men and women.
You are the only one, he said
in the light of eyes he couldn't see
pressed around him.
You are the only one, he said towards them
and against them
while engaged
with the animal
he kissed and licked,
and the dog licked his face, his hands,
his mouth.
You are the only one, he said
or didn't – You are the best one here,
aren't you?
and the lovely young men and women looked on
in distaste, fascination
to make them jealous.

.

Scabbed once-white tenements
set for demolition.
Tin, wood, nailed or stacked
where doors were.

Planted
in the street's centre –
tall
rough wooden posts.
Rain. Mud.

Back of this scene, part
of it, a
hall where
scattered
people

came: became
dancers, lonely, desperately
lonely,
thrown
into shapes

in a play of lights and shadows
out of themselves, a movement

(ghostly desire).

.

In dream she was after all in
Singapore, telephoning
to a painter
who used batik-dyes –

connection –   this was years before.

Colours,
colours of eyes   and
then buses, streets, shanty-dwellings.

Waters,   night
and colours of the eyes

open to all obscenity
and poverty –   the colours
flowing, stained through,

strongly, deeply   through

the immense surface.

.

Simplicity's table: to sit
clean-shaped metal jug
and cups, bowl of metal,
on plain table of wood.

Simple

until its death:
textures,
surfaces,
shapes,
moving,
changing.

> From exile, in
> exile: in exile a
> *lake of music.*

.

Figures,   dream and waking –
different faces   yet
there is commitment

even beyond longing.

How is this true?

An abstract development –

shocking, bewildering, perhaps,
or disappointing
to the sceptical
gentleman I worked for
(running messages, copying documents),

who remembered little paintings,
charming, "native" pictures.
This new thing, flowing colour,
disturbed. It wasn't like
the grubby,
astonishingly grubby, photos of women
shown to you in the streets,
or the pictures which moved on the streets,
postcards which moved as you drove into the lush countryside
where poverty, labour
and alcohol daily knocked
the "natives" out come nightfall.

This other thing wasn't recognisable.
But forget those travelled executives with weak,
wet handshakes:

elsewhere
a man with a tenor saxophone
is reshaping *All of Me*
with strength and grace;
he names it
Background Music,
it claims
my attention.

Three-Way

What stares still: gate? pillars
with tomb? monument? Certain:
stone; the image carries
grain,
(maybe) intensifies. Now if I move
closer it is part of a history broken,
several: geographic, personal,
cultural. If I pass flowers
purple on a neighbourhood fence
I come to my grandmother's garden
gate: she fifteen years dead,
my childhood blurred. I
come also to you, who bring
to bear
flowers in wild cut into the domestic
room, scene: table, glass, a garden out
the window in back. You speak
before me
but the words are elsewhere. Heard.
The gate closes in focus. I'd bring flowers
any distance
now if it
could be. For love stares
into the domestic-wild, light blinding
in the window. A man stopped painting
and grew roses for the years. What image now
is foundation, ground eye flies back to,
he had placed his paintings in a window-front
and it is a place in the heart isolated,
historical. Time
shares nothing but it breaks: my family
and others loved, years and distance separate;
they gather strangely to themselves in the shadows
of the hearth. So it is you have joined
past in distance, a past not your own; and come down pausing
at the window looking out and then come down
the stairs – and out the darkened hall

into day. In imagination you swim in foaming blue
water, your face laughing caught a moment in time.
Part,
even as it breaks the rest; part of the *unity*
another painter
tried to record (*not a solid block –*
nor separate things added together
like a necklace). His work anomaly; his death
a private sorrow. He sits in a kitchen
in half-light, haggard yet calm face, wise
aged eyes, hands joined on the table, still
image death bleeds towards total light or total dark, pulling
the forms into that obscurity of light or dark. Gate:
possible.

Audrie Browne

1.

Girl
all eyes, too tall for
her age,
sitting on a fence
throwing pebbles.
Older,

the knots,
nodes, of *when*
come to meet us: she rode into the town
on horseback –

days; strong summer heat.
She dismounted, to ask

directions. Left
the first man she met
writhing in the dirt, hands
clutching groin,
mouth working upon
the air. Went on
in search of a hotel.

(*Not* a gentleman, Audrie
thought, no
gentleman says a thing like *that*
to a
lady.)

2.

Gold body, gold-coloured clothes,
gold teeth revealed in a smile –
invited to the bar for a drink

he said, Golden Boy; call me
Golden Boy.

Later – he lounged on a grassy slope;
formal attire, cane. Petticoats,
he said.
Petticoats.

3.

At one end of town
Audrie waited,
disconsolate.

Around her
were signs:

a golden statue
poised on one foot
on top of the town hall;

a gold key
turning
in a lock.

4.

She gave him a toy,
a little bear
dressed
in a clumsy suit.

Listen, Audrie said to him, the child,
poor
idiot. Listen: I tell you this
only because you can't understand.
Gently
she placed

her hand
on his shoulder. Smiled.

Listen, she said. When
I was younger I believed
everyone strove for perfection,
that it was only time.
We were tested here, in
love, to achieve
the realm
of perfection.
But I cried,
she said, for ten years
for love. And the shapes –

absence throws the shapes
into empty doorways
all my life.

5.

At first sight.
Gleam
across the distance,
light striking
the golden body,

dude elegance
of perfected man
       shaped by hundreds of years
       of stupid insistence.
Smile caught
in memory's shutter,
flashing gold teeth –

Golden Boy. Audrie's hand
went straight for her revolver –

and the *present*
comes to meet us,
pebbles hitting earth,
and my friend calls sweetly to her –
the tall girl in the darkening garden –
to stop,
as we make supper
in his house
in a New Town near the sea.

A Sort of Beguine

1.

– Love takes care
of drugs
and the education of children –

the words (Campanella's,
The City of the Sun)
turn back
into endurance:

an English nurse in a small
Asiatic country
in wartime
wrote of one she loved:
    Sometimes she had taken
so many sleeping pills
that she didn't even recognize me.
She would either be sitting sadly in the café
or sleeping in the street.

2.

On a warm Spring day –
odour of blossoms along the avenues –
I went to my doctor
for a letter for exemption
from that same war.

    What are our choices –
our steps lose their way; our ground is lost.
Eyes stare out – stare past
what it was they held for their own.

      What are our choices,
if history
      is *a time that kills?*

3.

Hovels (sheet-tin); lights of
hurricane-lamps within.

Lord of the Worlds: what
are our choices? Light streams
at the wall, where we would stop –
except that the eyes have met
and they have not turned from each other.

4.

Seeing into the openness
of absence
and death – obscure,
irremediably dark –

the music of *decay and dismay*
is a sort of beguine.

There was a contact
endured in eyes: I leapt in.

                (For Liz Thomas and Steve Lacy)

Through Fire

1.

Playing his music
at the piano… the others
are gathered up
into admiration
and vision.

Heat licks the forms
(these people, the room
and its things)
into a glowing texture,
at which we could – say –
warm our hands;
except that it might
at any time break
into a fiery fragmentation –
every form blazing
and breaking apart.

2.

Listening to that music –
*its organization
of disparate materials* –
you saw how pale sunlight
fell everywhere in the garden;
regardless.
Small guileless face
framed by long blonde hair –
first glimpsed in a dark
street, her face lit up
as she walked, holding
the torch towards herself.
Eating snow. Looking through people
as if there were no one there.

Taking a hand to make that person
perform a task for her; then
abandoning interest again.
She sits in the garden and

what we hear is not only
the tragedy of man
but also the tragedy
of the elements, of the animals,
of the plants, of the stars....

3.

The eagle-headed, winged man
broods in a grey light
fixing his cruel features
in relief, his naked feet
stopped in their tracking
along the stone
corridor... now his
power's superseded and no
piling-up of bodies

can itself be equal
to that heat and flame
the human world
will not pass through:

which is endless
raging negation.

4.

Yet
   the intellect receives
a body of fire
and ranges through space,

leaving the soul to judgement.

Or: steam throws shadows
on the wall (thin branches
in wind). I stand
with a bowl – stairs behind
and door in front
but caught between, floated
or brushed onto the surface
of the wall: from which
to leap out again
in the next instant of perception.

5.

The hand lifts over the frame
of the car-window, child's arm
curved awkwardly in that gesture,
her mouth reaching to the boy's mouth.

The straightening of a girl's neck
as the eyes turn
to suddenness of light.

Broken sequences.
       …the
gravity of what is human, *deep within
the soul –*
      is loved,
but loved sorrowfully,
because of the threat of destruction
that constantly hangs over it.

We come back to the melody of it
andante, after the crashing chords
have prepared for its insistence.

There and Here
(Fragments)

The deepening late blue of sky appearing in the window-frame; blue juxtaposed with the green of curtains; blue, for nothing in glory, undiminished by the dirty surface of glass. Walking in Amsterdam – a sign reading 'AURORA' stopped me. I remembered what I had not remembered for years: the name I had given to the heroine of an early prose text, taken from the title of Boehme's *Aurora* just as Gérard had taken the name Aurélia from a story by Hoffmann.

*

In my own early prose texts I worked, out of Nerval and Lowry, with coincidence of events ("the linking-up of things") as the subject-matter, and with juxtapositions, interrelational linking or cutting, as "method". At the same time as this (1971 to 1972) I worked on a long essay on Nerval's work, especially on the images in *Aurélia*; and on a shorter essay on Lowry, which I revised for publication after coming to London in 1972.

In terms of working operations, I tended towards a direct handling of material, cutting up my texts and taping them back together in different combinations. With the Nerval essay, I depended upon chance findings in books I would take almost at random within a limited area of selection, from the shelves of the library at Melbourne University.

*

Without any warning, G— came and sat at our table in the Café Au Montmartre in Tottenham Court Road. My friend asked her about her dervish dancing lessons: Do you really whirl about? She said, No; she hadn't got that far yet. My friend and I moved on to the subject of coincidence – marvellous happening – in writing, as subject and as method. I talked about my apprenticeship as a writer, in Malcolm Lowry and Gérard de Nerval. Breton's *Nadja* and the *I Ching* came into the conversation too; though I have never really concerned myself with either, to be honest (which I wasn't). We had put the woman into a distance, which was a fake distance (I knew exactly where she was). "And through the glass window shines the sun": 6.15 of a winter evening, London, 30/10/75.

*

We were in a Greek restaurant in Notting Hill, and she was questioning me about the origins of my depression. What could I have said? That I grew up in a place that would make anyone aware of other possibilities depressed. Or that I grew up in a family whose members had almost no friends, in a household situated over a small brass-foundry that was operated solely by my father. Within that family I became conditioned to a brooding loneliness which I have never broken out of. Should I mention my early reading, the fact that I was immediately drawn to Nerval and Hölderlin, poets of loss and madness, whose visions helped to consolidate my own approach to a horizon, and the nature of that horizon? I am already sick of this particular story. I will only mention, for what it's worth, that I ended up telling my friend that I wouldn't be seeing her again. A terrible argument followed. And that leads to another story again.

*

"I have tried very hard", she wrote, "to understand and to destroy the barriers I have, naturally, against you (not because you are you but because you are another human being), but I can't do it, because I know you have so many weapons with which to wound me (and you do not use them sparingly). Only a fool or a total idealist throws himself into battle with no armour and no weapons and he probably gets destroyed."

The image. Upside-down, you're laughing; the motion of the swing's caught. The image caught: irresistibly; laughter in a face, an image catching me transversely; the motion of the swing caught, forwards, and reversed, here, to backwards.

*

He said: Suppose you'd loved someone and you wrote out of that. Suppose that. A boy staring out of the window into the night, figures moving casually in the street below. A radio on in the darkened and humid room, intense music.

This is an attempted destruction of my own beginnings.

*

I walked to the top of a terraced park to meet them; but at midnight we found ourselves at a café, lost, the poorly lit streets all alike. In the heat people lay down to sleep on the pavement or on top of parked cars. Through large square gaps left in the pavement we could see the sewers; someone told me of a man who fell down one of these holes during a storm and was found in a river across the other side of the city, dead. The woman (impeccable voice, impeccable manners, English, upper middle-class), said to me, Look at the cat, (a skinny cat, obviously underfed), why don't they feed it? The answer should have been self-evident. She wrote to thank me for my writing, saying it was wisdom. I am not that man. I am not that man, so, midnight, we found ourselves at a café, lost, the streets all alike. In the heat people lay down to sleep on the pavement. Some of them were not sleeping. They were sick, or decrepit; they couldn't get up.

The black oval surface framed in gilt,
from which I expected my image to return
during a city walk, unaccompanied by flowers,
fails. Catalogue the things evoking love
and evoking desire – the same equal things:
garden in night, pathway, train-station, shops
and cafés; the story binds them disparate.
We fail each other over and again
as if tumbling down a hillside, giggling,
screaming. Each lives to bear difference
which is endurance, on these streets
or in ghostly dream; equally: the face
fails to appear.

The stones at junctions
of dark streets or country roads
give comfort to lost children,
the sheets of rain, wind-swept,
tell them again
the stones' talk
quiet and obdurate,
insist and drive it home
and still insist. These
are the companions –
they say, Blood is red,
fire is red; they say: *It's a long*
road that's got no end,
it's a hard way that'll never change.

Set up on a hill: a structure
that the children of two warring factions
might come to play in –
become lost in, and find themselves home.

– I could never bring myself to go back,
he said, to the one place I ever felt at home:
how could I face those people, my terrible people,
after all the destruction and murder of war?

(For Mathias Goeritz)

Lights, openings.
Gulls wheel
in the evening sky;

crossing the bridge
of lights
we crossed over.

Only through
semi-opaque glass —

a bird on the ledge,
whose fluttering

shadow-shape's
sufficient against opening

the window to see clearly —
seeing nothing.

Burnished verticals
of the window's grid –
equality's drained
into the broken shining
of a single line.

Proximity of death.
Reminded
by light.

    (For my aunt)

Poem (for Paolo Uccello)

The landscape winds out
in black and grey washes,
colours
slowly seep into it, dream.
This was my youth:
the fields blue,
the cities red, and the buildings
in various colours.

Loving the birds most of all.

Rain

Rain occurs,
not as the entrance
into a story, as old poems might be,
but as fact.
Where the line curves into the distance
and the sound goes, there is a light
dim but certain,
a path of white stones
we didn't follow
that day or ever.

A dust storm obliterated
the afternoon light for an hour –
my mother was left isolated
in fear on the street.

Anterior dark
makes its claim upon light.

Poem
(for Faith)

Augustine in despair
beholds his own face
(his life); a child cries,
Take up and read. He reads;
he changes. I too turn
right round. Your face
before me rewrites my sight.

"Above the earth", she said,
"I am a virgin, within it, honestly, no."
It haunts their speech,
the boy and the girl.

They stood within
the miniature garden
looking at each other. She cried.
Why? he asked.
But she didn't know why.

Two birds flew up,
close to their faces.
Without their noticing,
night had fallen.

Ballad

1.

Sisters – who would come
singly to their house

or they would meet them in the streets.

 – They followed the road
into a forest
to a

clearing. Other people
had already gathered there in the

bright afternoon innocence gathered
for the meal.

2.

She came to the door
to ask for some tea, worn out
walking streets in search

of more substantial help. 'Past
her prime', the expression goes – yet
incredible sweetness in her words
her manner. The plan

of the dwellings was the 'plan'
of heaven as the designers saw it
& the plan substantially failed.

3.

The younger sister
seemed strong enough in herself
though she also drifted

having neither home nor
occupation & having left
her husband. The older

lived in fear of the man she'd
left, believing he burned her dog
in a furnace & desired
the same end for her. She'd come

to their house & having nowhere
to go home to, would try to stay
& once did. 'Don't use the towel she used'
they told the boy, their son,

after she'd left – & the concern cut in upon
his whole sense of position

of how he could stand in the light.

He collapsed, lay helpless
& the figure in white bent
over him: hand, arm working to mark
time, metronome, before the unforeseen –

the other man, standing alongside
in turn collapsed, on top & they lay
together, helpless –

the man in white
bent over them, lifted (hands, arms
working to lift): then
resumed his count. The figure on the floor
raised himself, but still helpless,
hopeless, hand clutching stomach, face
lifted to stare in
incomprehension. Two
faces
painted red, the blood.

'Then', said the girl, 'years
later when the winner had gone insane
the defeated man would visit him
in the asylum, bring him flowers –

'though', she added,
'it's almost too much to say it.'

– It is too much to say it.

The window frames
myriad events, world
seeping into a room

in a medley of times
and places: crazed dream
sustaining an anxious

brightness, that an Alberti
or da Vinci would wake from
fascinated, terrified. All

day the man sits on a bed,
his eyes fixed on the screen
of moving images. Then

he gets up, plays alto
for *lost life*, the sound
harsh and crying.

The Room

The perspective
of the room
is mirrored out

through the sky which
now is dark – darker
than deepest blue – and

the room's light
is caught like a flare
a painter's
given permanence.

On the mountain
dark green,
water poured amongst trees,
streamed
at the windows
of our vehicle.

Rain and mist:
the immeasurable.

                      (For John Levy)

Predestination – a painter gave me
and *chances,*
dark,

standing amongst
the flowers, how
do we endure in love.

. . . .

Sitting on steps – eyes closed,
my head bowed
in photographs.

City beneath a hill, blue
from the sea. Girls
at nearly every door in my street.

. . . .

Trying out the names,
buying yoghurt
from a street vendor –

night – small groups wandering.
Nothing out past, or within,
but ocean.

In the blue
broken also by a tree's
copper-red flakes
beyond table,
books and window –

the wild form of the cloud
closed into the perfect form of the bird's wings
sustains a Spirit
to speak, to bless.

(For Jennifer Durrant)

The surviving light
wavers
in dark: the dying fire's
its own wreath.

– Speak in a montage,
flame
against night; a broken
succession.

(For W.)

The Field

The holy stones are broken, and scattered in the field where orchids grow. Looking into the heart of the orchid – flower after flower – we recite those phrases that in our keeping survive.

(For Edouard Roditi)

Frescobaldi on the organ
mingles with the rain outside:
I picture them side-by-side/
overlapping/ superimposed –
where eye claims them over ear.

She came down a stairway, dark,
into the street to
a place of fountains.

The face close up
stops in its motion
in time, or almost so   .

It is slow if not
quite still
my eyes breathe in
what it says, what she

says in her eyes
so quiet
as almost silent.

for J. R. – i. m.

in the marketplace:
lanterns – &
children with fruit, who
call out
by the bright stalls.

time condensed & re-
composed, figures
scurry
in that space, movements
crossing & recrossing:

figures of myself
moving in the
sphere of love
      dark
a   dark
place there, a blur, a
shadow-site

where disaster has come;
a friend
dead: &
so the figures travel
in patterns
        dark, shock-
darkened, love knows.

perception (blue
bands of TV

over a river
image
      over –

on the telephone speaking
to a friend, viewing
as if he might be
in the next room

riverside dwelling
planks & other debris
in the river

      association, I said
isn't that what
you mean?   blue &
red
tints

2 about Music

the faces rows of faces
restless uncertain gazes
the faces flushed
with emotion
as the notes begin
the air pulsating

....

a love of glissandi
seemingly impossible
impossible too that song
endlessly extending
through layers
shifts and contrasts

so then turns away
just the head
that slight movement past
all possible recognition
whatever disfigurement or
face suddenly unwelcome to see

nothing in my life tells me
that this is inevitable
nothing either has such song as
your face your movements
your words pull the music slowly after them
and I follow you up the stairs
to a lighted room
where on a table the blue
flower grows in dirt

the taste of curds
in a dream was pleasing
even after she awoke
though it signified death
Perpetua awaiting that death
in the Roman circus prayed for aid
for her long dead
brother his suffering

Japanese *raku* bowl
deepness of black lacquer
obscurity
broken (shattered) with the red leaves
that fell from my tree
gold veins heal it now & cover
its black obscure face

what would it mean
I asked
to enter into the heart
of the snow
blue flame of the gas fire
showing red above the flame
enlarged motion to enter
they both have gone
(the darkened rooms)
outside it is snowing
twice in this winter
4 walls (white) interrupted
by a door
which opens onto night
darkened stairs
tomorrow evening
my friend will climb
to come into this room
sit, & talk
a white ceiling, a fire
in the room next door a girl
sleeps
in my own body someone
sleeping
one person
her blonde hair, her white
body
(what does it mean?)

Door of Paradise

A shattered colour-slide (steeple against blue of sky, clusters of dwellings, trees). It lies on the circular tabletop among numerous photographs in which one face remains constant – he had sought for an image of her, and found many.

When she was a child he told her stories. Now he's forced to listen to stories about her. – She walks in a trance, he thought, among those who will use her, and then wake her, for their pleasure, to cruelty and indifference.

.

All the doorways we passed through together formed a sequence, enduring over several years – doorways private and public; doorways repeated again and again, and doorways never passed through on a second occasion. And within that long sequence, gaps, marking diverse separations. For she would stop seeing me, caught up at first in parental objections; later, when she had broken with her family, in the fluctuations of her own perplexity.

.

Night: a wall appeared; uprooted and trodden ferns.

And it is proper to have pity for God: so I have heard; so I believe.

.

A line of treetops caught at him. Poverty; urgency. Where the branches end in a final crown of foliage, bloodshed's diminished by each glimmer of light. He is shaken; and these poor trees, that also possess nothing, cry out as what he sees.

•

In a dream, I was with him at a small fairground within sight of the sea. He had shown me a letter:

> I remember that day in Florence when we stood gazing at the gilded bronze doors of the Baptistery; at the Door of Paradise especially, for its splendour. What did all those Biblical stories, each held in an image, hold for me? – Oh father! It's *not* a door – it's a solid wall of gold!

It made me angry. – It's not hers, I said. He was shocked; he didn't believe me. – Damn you, I said; it's not even her handwriting – is it? But he only looked away, so that he faced the sea.

•

A childhood memory: metal trees surrounded by sand. – A *dream*? someone may ask. Tell them nothing, don't elaborate or explain; your hand, the wrist bandaged, brushing back your long hair the wind continually disturbs.

Or else tell them there's still the choice of refuge; or a consuming fire out of the bramble.

Legend

The yacht (he said) had twelve drunken poets on board, and when they sighted land they all dove into the sea to swim the rest of the way, and had to be pulled out again.

.

Lines are drawn across or down, or up to lift gaze and smile: as yours are lifted now in the wet and darkened street.

I think of the painter Jay DeFeo, standing full frontal and naked to the waist in the middle of the eyes she'd drawn huge in pencil line.

Do you also stand within the image; is there a story to tell? The affective lines descend and ascend, from your eyes to your pudenda and to your eyes.

.

– And your writing's at an impasse, too! the woman flung at him, at the end of a series of accusations. They sat together in an area bruised to the extent where friendship loses its purchase.

Some months later, he had a dream in which he traced the whereabouts of a singer he'd long admired on the evidence of a few recorded songs of almost thirty years ago. He'd feared a story of alcoholism or drug addiction to account for those years; but when she and her grown son met him at the station and drove him to their house, he found he couldn't believe the supposition to be true of her. – Why, he eventually asked, did you only record those two albums? – I've made other recordings, she told him; it's just that you haven't heard them.

.

Formless yet complete. One register's juxtaposed with another; there are erasures and connecting lines; marginalia.

> young woman
> in front of me
> nothing speaking
> between us
> like the distance speaks
> rows of trees
> mist and rain

…form dissolved into feeling.

∙

We were remembering events from the past, which had happened in a distant country where we'd both lived. In my late adolescence (I said) I would sometimes catch sight of a young filmmaker who resided in the same house as one of my friends. He was praised for a film that combined animation with live footage, occult symbols with shots of a young woman naked on his bed. One evening I entered the hallway of the house as he was shouting at this same woman, telling her to get out, that he'd finished with her; he was on the landing, and she stood on the stairs below. Her look of pain spreading through disbelief as ink through water caught me; it still catches me – while his film remains as a mere schema.

∙

– The heart's affection is enmeshed in vicissitude.

– What's most real is that which we never know, yet there – mid-point, invisible – constancy comes to find itself.

Inscribe these lines beneath a portrait, in which the eyes' impress and the mouth's disposition evoke a perpetual vigil.

At the Heart of the Thicket

On the walls there are many images. In order to be here, they floated across the water, never getting wet. They *speak by themselves* to visitors.

•

The spirit is good *but the flesh is weak*, my mother wrote to me, *isn't that the saying.*

•

– Why don't you ever talk to people? Why sit by yourself like this each day, in the same tiny arbour?

– Why do you keep watching me?

I overheard two art-school students talking nearby; one said: I went up to that girl in the dirty white dress over there, and she *smelt*. She –

But I closed my ears to what else they had to say. (I'd seen both students walking in the cloisters and at tea in the refectory, parading their clothes spotted and streaked with oil paint.)

A sparrow inspected the grass for leavings, near the exposed, ophidian tree-roots.

•

The woman speaks of her friend, an aging, married man, priest-like in manner and belief, who waited at a college party, so out of the usual, for his young student; and danced with her, a slow dance with glissades, creating a passage through all the people surrounding them.

•

Through the windows of the airplane, the mountains emerge from clouds – monstrous and beautiful in their enormity, their formations; conjuring fear much as a person's presence may bring fear. But with a person, the impress of that fear can be especially deep when he or she is someone you love.

•

At the other end of the park, a dumbshow lecturer stands in the midst of a group of students sitting on the ground. I can only see his gestures, I hear nothing at all: *does* he, in fact, say anything? The figures are small in the distance. There is nothing but two long expanses of grass, separated by a path of stones and earth, between them and where I sit; above us, there is the sky, which darkens.

•

A small group of teenagers, two boys and two girls, lounge around the entrance to the station. As I walk past and look their way, one of them – a tall, strong-looking black youth – grabs the girl beside him by the throat, forcing her against the wall. She catches my eye, and laughs.

•

— You collected the bones and skulls of men whom the law courts had put to death, thinking you were the better for defiling yourselves at their graves.

'Martyrs' you called the dead men, and 'ministers', and 'ambassadors' from the gods to carry men's prayers.

.

Waiting at the entrance of the passage for the truck to drive past, they didn't quite face each other yet neither did they quite turn away; leaves and rain blowing at their faces. Later, they would come to exchange words and gazes.

Wind in the branches of heavy foliage; thoughts struggling with contrary thoughts. Liquid begins to form in the air; then to fall; and, where it has fallen, to soak in or flow off; and, even if colourless, to stain.

She appeared to him in a dream, and said: *I am pursued like a wolf from the sheep. I am not a wolf. I am word, and spirit, and power.*

.

Blue crystal. At the centre of the thicket.

.

A house that you reach by a series of narrow lanes past the seafront. Inside, a door opens upon weeping, bleeding, speaking, in their variety of colours.

Dark Ground

(for Brian Louis Pearce)

The other people there wanted to talk about art; he didn't.

There was a glint of hysteria in his eyes. He said: It was a vast secret society, calling itself the Agapé. Its leaders authored the Christian Gospels, and circulated them for their own worldly ends. They assassinated those whose power they coveted. Montanus wanted to reform the Agapé; he was condemned at Rome, and committed suicide….

.

A woman and a man sit down on a bench by a pond – to talk, earnestly. No sooner have they come to the point of their conversation, than two children commence tricycling around the bench; then a young man asks to have his picture taken. (She smiles, and photographs him.) Finally, another woman sits down beside them. So they leave, continuing their talk as they wander through the park…. She says: We should have met then; by which she means, nearly two decades before – when things would have been possible.

.

– I keep looking at my notes, but not doing anything with them, I said.

He said, Why don't you burn them, and start from nothing?

– Good God, no! I said.

I watched the pebbles plunging into gelatinous water, its colour a pale olive-green.

Whatever you may chance upon, has already existed, Tertullian wrote; *whatever you have lost, returns again without fail. Nothing perishes but with a view to salvation. The whole, therefore, of this revolving order of things bears witness to the resurrection of the dead.*

Theology informs us in excess, where epigraphy instructs us in too little.

Heads emerge from dystopian holes in the ground.

– The naked bulb doesn't emit any light; but across the room, light comes from another bulb hidden beneath a shade....

I felt the necessity for some other rede, equal to the pressure of ineluctable loss.

A shepherd and his son witnessed my friend excavating in a remote area, and pitied him and his fellow archaeologists for the penance God had imposed on them. This friend dreamt that he alighted from a bus at the same stop as a young woman playing disjointed phrases on a harmonica – phrases that became more and more frenzied. A short time later he saw her again, as she plunged down from a high building; and her body lay bleeding and lifeless on the ground.

Someone is poised at the door, divided by thoughts of going in and of staying where he is. Wilful hero, he bears an engraved bracelet to remind him of lions that were slain. But I think of the procession of poor, variegated beasts, *bleached, gilded, or empurpled.*

– All my fear rises up; and it is not for him, but for you. Don't linger in this place, dear.

.

A slow accretion of memories; a darkening expanse of water. The darkening ground.

.

Remembering… her face, her movements, her words that pull the music slowly after them; and the music is as modest and penetrating as a Dowland ayre or a Machaut ballade. Remembering, too, how I followed her up the stairs to a lighted room, where on a table the blue flower grew in dirt.

>   her voice entering
>   the room's space
>   eases anguish and
>   with that ease
>   ipseity's ruptured
>   through the break
>   I can attend the words
>   long-distance as they
>   glisten in darkness
>   forming an envelope lost
>   like an inset

.

On the notebook's cover a girl stands in a ballet-costume, her face covered in white make-up. Her hands gesture to the sky, an arc indicating lost and soteriological spaces. A secret society calling itself by love's name? I keep thinking of the woman whose ecstatic utterances were nothing the churchman could challenge with argument, leading him to resort to a third type of utterance: exorcism. The woman's followers stopped him from completing the act; yet he had won, all the same. A ring was unknowingly dropped in the dark. Beneath the night, the ground's caked and bleached.

.

Sitting down on the stone, you speak the fragments enclosed as dark within dark.

For Patty Waters

We were coming down from the top of First Mesa, after visiting an old Hopi woman who lived there; we could hear the singing clearly, even if nothing of the ceremony was visible to us. We'd known from the signs along the road that we weren't allowed to see the sacred dancing, but had decided to go, regardless, to the woman's village. A little girl came up to us and said very politely: Excuse me, non-Indians aren't allowed here during the Kachina Dance; then she skipped past us down the dirt track.

.

    …remember
    a child's variation
    upon trance

    there are souls
    it was said
    whose faults are as if written

    on paper in a dream
    the yellow-haired girl and I
    stroll by the water's edge

    there's a small wound
    at her wrist
    she mimics the geese's cries

    as we walk in their midst
    and they lift their wings
    to slap against the cold air

    there are souls
    whose faults are as if written
    on sand for the wind

•

While we were driving through the desert, away from First Mesa, I began to talk about a singer I'd long admired, whose work had been severely marginalized; indeed, it was all-but-forgotten.

Spare, reticent, tender melody was certainly present in her singing, but it would give way to an athematic exploration of sounds that couldn't always be plotted within conventional pitch-notation — and these often seemed extended from such as sighs, moans, screams, cries, shouts. Wistful, passionate, sad, anguished, joyful, serenely resigned, or enraptured. A voice that sometimes appeared to ride on the merest breath, could assume an intensity that evoked a fierce wind. Visited, ecstatically; as part of a *serious game*, a *sober inebriation*. For her distinction was also in the way that her singing took on all the colours of a devotion that passes through the stations of self-abandonment.

Suddenness, transverse.

Devotion

I awaken
from a dream;
irregular small
gaps glowing
phosphorescent
in the dark floor.
      Children's backs
are bent, their
faces masked by
grotesque ugliness
and age. They dance
around a fire on which
the men pour petrol,
pile branches; sparks
blowing all the distance
to where we watch.

Purity's
the needle's word,
I said; and
now that word
becomes sun and water
to pierce me.
      A reflection
of lights steadfastly
breaks apart. You pull
the edge of the water
over your breasts, then
further upwards
until only a curled lock
of blonde hair shows
from the sheet of it.

Massed shapes
of cacti
along the road.
Tree-tops – dark clouds –

odd-angled
on branches like wire.
   Her visage
a black featureless
cloth, the woman
murmurs *Fool –
you're a fool*; the voice
from that *magic box*
following her eccentric
path through
the night. I shake
blood from my fingers
in a small slow rain.

Voices
in the hotel's
hallway beat
across the bed
where you lie naked.
   A crown daisy
beside you. Doors
and windows are blue
in your eyes' sway.
Your excesses in devotion
to love, against every
hurt inflicted on you,
break perfection apart;
reason's heavenly city
is shattered
into shining debris.

The eagle
spreads its pinions,
sudden impatience
for flight
stirring in its body.
   The *kerygma*
travels through the air
from the mountain

above us, assuming
my friend's voice.
He speaks
of *the one pearl*
which is in the midst
of the sea; of those
unequivocal bonds
we daren't sunder,
unless all harm
should be shaken loose.

From a dream
of a black marble head
whose features
elude me, I wake
in an island hotel.
        Orange trees
along the front;
planks and litter
in the water. I dreamt
the truth, also:
that my hands were incised
deeply with patterns
never to be removed.
If in any life
I saw you from a distance
I'd hurry, drawn on by love,
to meet you.

Focus

With quickened attention,
your eyes find their way
past the appearance
of uniform vistas,
stacked masses of snow
on the mountain. Or you locate
someone sitting in a café,
shoulder-length blonde hair, leather coat,
cigarette; she says,
Eyes which fear death
forever flit from one pleasing face
to another; they'd replace
the living features
with a god's bronze image
of Classical perfection,
and let the empty sockets
keep their gaze. One by one,
you pick out the small foci of concern;
from the rounded ungainly heaps
covering rock shapes
another picture emerges.

*Attention is the rarest and purest form
of generosity.* Ruins, where so many
were slaughtered: rocky crevices
and sparse vegetation give as a keepsake
an image of skulls. Her eyes, *the hue
of the void, expressionless sky,
of shadows on far-off hill and cloud,*
plunge through monotonous heaps of snow;
or turn to you
as she speaks. Her voice
sceptical; wistful.
She says, Sweat aspires
to starlight; ache, passion,
arch into distances. Together
you'd seen photographs of the dead

attached to headstones. But dotted
along the mountainside, within
the restlessly winding terrain,
are places
of refuge,
shrines and monasteries.

Framed in the corner of a room
yellow with light, the woman
looks into the distance
in which snow is falling;
like a child whose eyes
are fixed upon the statue
of a lion, guardian spirit,
its mouth curled open in a grimace.
Fragmentary, mask-like
Aphrodite image –
as water to its own movements –
suffers awakening for you,
when you place its photograph
next to the woman's face
so each discloses the other's
alterity. Large eyes
beneath a fringe, slow
water movement of nerves.
Holes like black almonds,
entrances in the symmetry
of the poignant bronze.
Snow covers the stacked roofs,
the red-lacquered doors
are openings for you.

String-harmonics claim stillness.
What if Kuan-yin
were standing there,
to guide you home, in mercy
and compassion –
as much at ease in beauty
as the sculpted-wood figure,

whose eyes elide contact
with your own. The woman
holds a glass in one hand,
her cigarette in the other.
Her voice enters a distance
of telephone conversations,
telling you again
of the gods who suffered death;
of the head whose features
she saw in a dream,
falling into a blur;
of the white ruins
that once were the polychrome
temples of the Greeks.

Lost in contemplation –
she re-emerges from that sea
as if coming alive for the first time,
eyes widened, glistening.
She says: The one face
that substantiates
each face you address,
terrifies
beyond sight and words
when you fear death
and undivided darkness.
You hold her face
in double focus
with deepest darkness;
like *the double sensation*
of looking into a dark
interior space and out
into the landscape,
that you found in a painting
fiercely polychrome.
Likenesses float between
her face and the dark.

Faces

We didn't foresee that the dog
would follow us up the hill,
wheezing horribly; black
against the green and brown
of vegetation and mud. Spoken to,
simply, it followed a course
we didn't dictate. Did you foresee
how the child would react,
or merely provide
a certain light
to guide her?
Uncertain image, the light
startled within, palpitating –
she faces herself
as unfaced
victims face us
from an inherited past
of photographs, films, paintings.
Yet she strikes – somehow –
free of whatever tangles,
knots; and is loosed
into a different world.

We reached
sky, and the house at the hilltop
whose door opened from mud.
Among the sunlit tea trees,
and in the room where
my friend's small daughter
dragged her shy sibling
to see me,
memories were tesserae,
that reassembled.

There are faces
that have darkened like
frangipani petals

turning brown at the touch.
Others hold a light
in the constancy of which
I see illumined
the child facing her image
on a video screen,
and the tesserae
reassembling still.

The Park
(to the memory of F. W.)

The music, blues
on alto, occurs
where willow leaves
stir in the wind.
The line of notes
twists upwards to end
in a cry. Light and air,
and moisture in the air,
are a web threading
bushes, trees and benches
and the people
within the park.

The rhythm
is slowed, then
quickened again; line
shattered by anguish –
for the other
who suffers, dies.
And there are surfaces
on which tears have formed
from out of the air.
A cascade of
leaf and shoot
weeps; is all I see.

The siren
from an ambulance
brings the exterior world
to this park
stricken with music.
The web's a setting
for wings that flash,
and encompasses
affliction, death.
A gem of water
appears
on the back of my hand.

South London Mix

(for Lawrence Fixel)

At the corner of a church entranceway, a girl sleeps against a wall, in a squatting position, with her legs drawn up and her arms around them, head down on her knees. She is lightly dressed, with cotton T-shirt and frayed blue jeans. Her feet are bare, and brown with mud.

It comes on to rain.

.

       There are rooms,
       rooms leading to further rooms,
       joined together
       like an endless road.
       You could lose yourself
       in these interiors....

       I sit with a woman
       in a room at night.
       We talk
       about poetry. As the night progresses
       the room darkens about us,
       the air cools. Inside:
       there are windows and pianos.
       Outside: distances manifest themselves
       in roads like black tape
       interrupted by the occurrence of ponds.

.

I am haunted by the absence of meetings. – Meetings made impossible by deaths – such as those of Godfrey Miller and Roy de Maistre. Or the cessation of meetings, either by ruptured friendship, by the intervention of distance, or again by death. There are interiors I will never sit in, and interiors I will never know again.

°

Aeolian harp, or chimes of some sort (as we had in the room I first slept in, for a few weeks, in South London), that the wind sounds when a window is open.

Imagine the exterior of a house as being sensitive as someone's skin.

The "outside" penetrates what's "inside", if not physically, then in one's sense of a human environment.

What I am saying is obvious. *And* essential.

°

There were white patches left primed but unpainted on the blue ceiling, and when the door was ajar, if you were passing or about to go in, you often got the illusion of a room with the sky as its ceiling.

°

The stain-shapes, ochre, at the bottom of the porcelain sink, sometimes remind me of lovely moths, or rather, the imprint of a moth's life upon another, inorganic presence (as upon celluloid; think of Brakhage's *Mothlight*: though that was not really a film I much liked).

°

The clothes, drying (hopefully),
have become anonymous
white shapes
in the dark yard below.
Not thinking of insects,
earlier I drained boiling water
there from my food.
The clothes, full of dampness
and themselves, have
as their habitation the cold air.
I have temporarily lost them to the air,
to the condition of stones.

.

It used to lie in the centre of the garden, a long ochre-orange rectangle bordered neatly by the green of the grass and weeds. She's moved it since. Part of it's draped over the marble-white stone we sit on, near the top of the garden, and it's to one side also (the left), a small fern falls across it.

.

Clothes-lines describe and define a certain type of space in much the same way as a naked body and its particular movements do.

.

I dream your name, you are there, you are not there, the polished teak quietly snows.

.

He took us briefly into a room where another young man (a friend of his), his sister and an older woman sat together at a table. There were not any introductions. The older woman was a redhead with a face as clear-cut as a Modigliani carving, and quite beautiful; I saw her with a clarity in place of the vagueness of perception that shyness usually gives me in strange places. She laughed and said hello, and then he and I turned and went out of the room again, into another (smaller) room.

.

You get up in the early hours woken by a need, then you wash in the dark, in the water-light.

The woman stands in the foreground, straight, head high, but as if she's about to move. *She traps drops of liquid under the clear perspex face of a turntable.*

The others seem less important somehow. She's off-centre, to the left, and there's another to the side of her, but partly behind her, you hardly see him.

To the left, in the far corner, another woman bends forward, the weight of her body pressing towards the floor. To the right and further back are two men, one half-lying, half-risen, the other on his haunches, but with his head pointing downwards.

It's too early, you go back to bed.

.

String unwound from her mouth. Or clouds. Floating out.

Drinking. Cups. Blue smoke.

And earth; and light:

·

Brief flash of sunlight across the eyes, bringing one into a different (almost non-visual) space for a second or two, before seeing oneself reflected in the glass of the door.

·

There	in
the	room
suddenly	brightness.
Suddenly	red
floor,	yellow
walls,	white
door.	There.

·

Semi-opaque glass: an area divided with vertical lines. Muted colours of the gray doorstep, the entrance-path, the street, the sky: horizontal whites, browns, greens, blues, all muted. Water.

·

      Kitchen door open
      to the possibility of rain.
      Walking out into the garden,
      the house open to this possibility,
      I think of concepts, abstract
      paintings, soundings of a pond.
      I think of death. The luminous
      edge of life/death – the oblique –
      appears more readily, at times,
      at times of rain. The house
      takes on other colours.

....

> Reprieve: sun shining, yet cool.
> Furniture showroom in Clapham:
> uninviting, canned, cold for a cold mind,
> pathetic
> luxury. My aunt's house, showrooms
> from thirty years ago. To walk into it
> is to walk into a house out of time, out of touch.

•

A packet of stone-ground wholemeal biscuits, fawn colour, circular with indented edges, piled on top of each other into a column, protected and topped by a sheath of cellophane. It sits on the ledge, above the paraffin-heater, and in front of the Italian postcards (the angelic "little loves" of Rimini Cathedral, and the gold, red and white altar of St. Tripun Cathedral), amidst bottles, toiletry (soap and so forth), but in a space of its own, separate. It looks like a stand for a Brancusi sculpture. It is dwindling fast: the biscuits taste good.

•

The task is not even to get a sense of mystery into commonplace things again. I think the job is to reassert the value (and value is not mysterious exactly, *nor* magical, but intangible), of ordinary things. And in doing so, find the place where tangible and intangible meet, and concrete and abstract do likewise.

Again, about simple things: someone once said that a certain line in a poem of mine, 'Briar-Cup', was very beautiful. The line was: *Birds flew over the river.*

•

The wind moves the door a little. It opens onto the lower staircase, leading to the entranceway. The lock of the door is a square of worn black interrupted by rust-marks; the handle is of brown wood, blackened at the top, and with a few specks of white paint. The door was once, I guess, painted white or light gray, but this has been sandpapered down to a milky haze, irregular, over the pale brown wood. I listen to music (Jobim). I want to say something about attention.

•

"Turn quickly on to a floured board, knead lightly for a second only, and then turn into a greased loaf tin. Bake in a brisk oven for three-quarters of an hour."

I hear that the bread which looks at him / heals the hanged man, / the bread baked for him by his wife.... (Paul Celan)

•

The table: a grace. Though I'm not sure what it is to you, who have people here, family and friends, visitors, at table several days a week, maybe more than once a day, to cooked meals. For me it's something out of the ordinary. And the talk: *so*.

•

> The easy thing: friends
> care for nothing that has to be
> ripped from the other, the hard
> answer, the demand
> that truth be the hawk's truth.
> Not the "long haul", and not the flash
> of awakening, the rise of ecstasy:
> but / a shared and gradual
> intimacy.

2.

Guest. Was. Like. Ladybug. He. Garden. Would. Ground. He would. Gently. Place. A. Like. Leaf. Lived. Pond. Whose. Names. Man. Names. Carefully. And. Played. Friends. With. Children. Us.

I. The invitation was. Shy. Wore. To. Gray. Playfully. Buttons. Glass. On. Aging. Quiet. This man.

Was. Game. One. Inconsequential rules, and. Tea. Talking together for. Brief. Several. Writing. Grass.

•

It occurs in certain films, where in domestic scenes there is an isolation of certain moments.

•

My image of tao *is not a continuous road but just many dots.* (Toru Takemitsu)

•

Hands. Cloths. Covers. Tables and beds.

Bowls.

And

This.

And

The fish that.

On.

Lift up from.

Same.

In.

w,h,e,n w,e a,r,r,i,v,e,d h,e w,a,s m,a,k,i,n,g

Chanting. Cymbals.

Steel dots.

Orange, red, purple, green, yellow dots.

Leaves spilling water. Mushrooms; grass.

Arrived. We. Purcell. Making. He. A. Fire. When we. Saying. Next. Which. Hear. Described. Hand. Given. Daughter. That. Told. Conversation. Whole. Wished. Listen. Talk. Who. This. Had. See. Late. Two. At. Christmas. Him.

Friend. Upon. Later. You. Attention. Table. House. It. Go. Kitchen. Looked. And. Early. My. Visit. Area.

3.

suddenly (Ashvaghosha)
:*without beginning* (Fa-tsang)
:*without awareness* (Chen-chieh)

Youre two eyn will sle me sodenly (Chaucer)

.

Heart-bowl. Base and sides red.

We dip stumps into it.

.

Dream on a ridge

.

Between black and white, and colour – or rather black and white at the beginning of changing, – or would it be the other way, that the colours were at the penultimate stage of disappearing? – It was neither (or both), the image suggesting tints which never quite became evident, mainly a red washed out to a sharp faintness.

.

Between the switch of my water-heater and my table, six paces away, the needle-pricks of a sea make me focus further than before – further than the eraser behind my typewriter, further than the draped glass a few inches away from that. Between these, there is a pile of photographic negative, six or seven strips of it, whose subjects no longer interest anyone. On a diagonal of two feet away, there is a photograph, and this corresponds to what the sea evokes at this moment – a ghostly sea, because it's not there before me, but with the sharp points of light pricking its skin, pricking the eyes.

The sea evokes a woman, and there's nothing out of the ordinary about that. Evokes a way of standing in a room (which is not mine), of standing in a dress, the dress draping the floor it's so long, a way of having the arms and hands, not down at the sides, but at the waist, the hands clasped in front, and as if to have something but not to have anything, but at rest, and a way of holding the head, up and slightly to the side, the eyes a little nervous.

This space, between the light-switch and the table, corresponds to the space between the strips of negative and the photograph, and this is what I am left with.

.

Water. *And then I had to look at it, really look at it. Look at water.* Movements of it, in air, along surfaces, and over itself. And movements of air on water. Stairway, clear.

Time and perception. And perception like water.

.

Numerals. On a glass ruler. – Underneath, what? – Water, again.

.

This pond, this water… its movements (not *movement*) are lines moving past you, and past, past; and the motions in this circle which is at night so dark and somehow (paradoxically) still, draw you with them, yet you remain where you are as they stream past, ripples in a pond, and the ducks float further from immediate vision. These movements are constant, various, and probably indeterminate; paradoxically there is a stillness. Lines across smooth skin, moving across it, radiating….

At the bottom of the pond a hundred alarm-clocks rust into decay, waiting for the time when they will burst into water-lilies, or strange night-flowers for the blind.

.

…the piano wandering and reflecting within its own huge solitudes.

.

Running down from the tap onto the basin bottom, the water makes a circle that quivers and metamorphoses.

It makes a hole. Like a hole in the sky; a hole in light; a hole in your shadow, whereby I glimpse the womb-warm dreams. My fingers search for portholes.

.

Cloth against skin;
bone and muscle hold to a grace
and a power.
Comb on dresser; letters; on
the floor a weaving-loom:
colours for cloth,
lines that intersect and
move, move and intersect.

Night. Skin: skin.
Face: face. Eyes:
eyes. Cheek: cheek.
Hair: hair. Shoulder:
shoulder. Teeth:
teeth. Waist: waist.

Breasts: breasts. Hip:
hip. Arms: arms.
Hands: hands. A

casual litany, each thing
answering to itself.

•

A psychotic Indian sculptor I met told me that a piece of soap was like a diamond: it cut.

•

A carbon of this one night, a negative of this one day.

•

Darning needles. Crochet needles. Knitting needles. Boot-maker's needles. Sewing needles. Pine needles.

•

Beneath and through us there is a flowing. Nausea; cliché. Stench: sweat and mess that are attendant.

•

The speech of dead birds troubles me. Their speech is like that of a woman whose life was once shattered, and who begins to grow old. The moons look heavy and durable, but they disappear like soap bubbles at the edge of a street.

·

My present boots are the tough sort, hiking boots that is, and made of leather. Which is rare. I avoid wearing leather, just as I avoid eating meat and fish, but I needed shoes or boots, and a friend gave these to me.

Is there anything else to say? – Only that boots (through walking) link up with stones, and stones link up with holes – ruptures, breaks, entries. But that's perhaps to say too much.

·

In a matter of seconds the green-stemmed, purple-flowered thistle changed in colour to a dull speckled bone. It approached the brick which lay almost in the centre (in width) and at about a sixth of the length of the garden. I used to regard this brick as an object for measuring distances with. But now it's nearly covered over with the debris of deaths.

·

All through the concert I heard the sound of blood beating as if in the distance, yet amplified greatly.

Suddenly a forest broke through the floor.

·

>   Waiting-rooms. But often
>   a park, with prior glimpse of her
>   at a window arranging flowers
>   as I walked past. Or a friend's
>   house, nearby. And the car where we sat
>   outside her home, one in the morning,
>   friends insisting that nostalgia demands
>   its vigils and attendances. Garden
>   and car: flowers and petrol;
>   and rooms that lead to other rooms,
>   waiting that leads again to waiting,
>   poems that lead to more poems....

    ·

Each day or night, quiet, the manner and conversation charming and polite, the people kind –

That night after I had found out about the hurt and the bitterness, the betrayals, beneath that talk, that quietness, that charm – I wandered the streets sick with a dull, tired anger. The figures on posters were suddenly disquieting, rage-provoking. I thought I was back in Melbourne. I walked along Oxford Street, and then down Bond Street to the Green Park Underground. The hard streetlights ached in the night. I didn't want to let go of that quietness, that kindness, those people. And I was sick with my own desire, my innocence, my own hurt and bitterness.

    ·

Knots. Tea. Breeze. She. It does. It does exactly, as she would and as she does. The breeze is cool, maybe a little more than you'd like.

Alcohol spilling suddenly, copiously, implausibly, over the photograph. Like the destruction of a world.

Again the Pleiades have come out.

This is a sentence. This is also a sentence. This is not a sentence.

•

Janet said this would be the last day we would know. Of course, we didn't believe her. But sixty-two hours have passed since then, and it's still the same day. No one knows how long it will last. The shopkeepers at Clapham South have not closed all this time. Will anyone die? I read Gordon Bottomley and, walking on Clapham Common, reflect on astrophysics and mycology.

•

She walks with difficulty, crosses your path, shuffling, but with deliberation – asks excuse for "embarrassment", asks (blood spots on her hands, breath rank) for a fare with which to travel – where? Do we get anywhere, or do we continually leave and come back?

My friend spends too much time in consumer meal bars; he needs vegetables badly – has a vitamin deficiency. His instinct plays up, and he snuffles grass, drooling, without any idea why he's doing so.

I am tired of the way decencies keep erasing themselves.

•

Photostat hands. Grain. Stet. The imprint of newspaper on wood. Lines on glass: splinterings, cracks, engravings. Things stay. And things disappear. Edges, margins, horizons. Strips of wood. Meeting- stopping-places. Juttings, hoverings, borders. You ride past. Cuttings. The air. Back. Where there is always a sky. Things that go and things that stay. Edges of memories. Of memoirs. Alphabet. Almost. Mossy. Small shining modes. Lace on wood. Deaths occur also. Fragilities / temporality. Precisely.

Counting. And there are wings. There are, then, the two things: numbers that you count, and the old man's voice that soars and rides like a bird in air. When you are in love with these things. In the city there is no space, there is only accumulation and gaps. Space becomes a reality again: elsewhere. Stones give you space: space you. Give stones; upset, you set up stones.

The Flamingos

1.

Like the everyday notation of stars/ there is sickness;
on the paving-stones rain falls as discontinuous footfall. Easily,
and talk enters loneliness in that way, talk that can be written down,
talk that can't be written down.

There is in the voice a pressure that compounds
gentleness and blood. Where there is a sky
there is also a table, hard and resistant
to the hands that push down on its surface.
Our voices draw unasked-for respect from the air.

2.

There is nothing to answer to the word purity
except in reproach. Purity is the needle's word.
The heart wishes for certain moments;
the rain lies in puddles on the stones.

As a thing I can't separate from this struggle
to get a situation down exactly,
there occurs to my mind a flock of pink flamingos,
beautiful and threatened
by the indeterminacy of the approaching night.

The Same Again
(for John Pauker)

The pressure behind what we
say and do
(fortunately inconstant)
is a whole history
and it is bruised.

She stopped part-way up
the stairs then
and turned.
The movement of a little
memory is part of a slow
flood only; at times
the entire vision is inundated
in a gush of illumination:
of cold or warmth.

Upon the stairs
talking to someone
who is following:
her blonde hair
illuminated by what light
there is. Don't speak
of the moments
as burning as candle-wax
burns beneath the flame,
the bright figure of
delusion.

The Cups

From the cups
I poured the
black and the white
together,

the liquids,
into one cup

then back
into two.

Then they
were one
but in two

and we drank them.

Half-turned away through our half-
failure of recognition, the angel's

gigantic form hovers – the wall
hovers – as flame, within

dreams' scribbled dark. Flawed work:
a life's architecture of fault.

Lacunae
(for Mathias Goeritz)

We sorted through the stars,
bag after bag of them,
for the message that was ours:
it read death.

The stars passed through our fingers,
we were left with death;
they were arranged in constellations
of concrete around a wooded lake:
one man had seen the lacunae
as possibilities
in life's favour and beyond life and favour.

Vermeer

She sits intent, alone. Her hands are artful, her head bowed.

She sleeps at a table of fruit, she dreams, the fruit dreams and the table also, the door is open and light shines on the bare threshold. The other chair is empty. It faces her.

Only the servants of the house are visible.

Inside, in the room a window is open. He looks up from the charts, the light is softly upon his face.

The heavy gray drapes have been drawn, for a time. The window is open. The fruit and rugs are again on the table, by which she stands, facing the window. She reads the letter. Sadly.

Her intent fingers artfully, carefully move needles. The red thread trickles and dangles off the canvas.

The burning wood says:
"Warmth spells destruction."
Pebbles glitter and glow
in an ancient, irrevocable
sea. I am dice
cast by this light-
and-dark of the ocean's
blades. The mind a box
sunk in it,
an eye peers out
of a hole in the box.
The eye may be kissed.
The flash of death
can be as many things
as the world.

Beech furnishes the
room, it brings me to a place,
I sit on ash,
bewitched by the lines
drawn from silver
birch. The forest has been called
into employment,
the trees are strung with
crossing strands, the gleam
of a brooch made when you were
walking that way one morning,
leads you home.

An afternoon with a circus:
with dream-owls,
with Chinese shadow-figures,
with a Shepherd of Clouds
for Ringmaster.

And his wife painted
shyly and humbly
but with conviction,
painted and wove
the clear colours and
shapes.

Baobab, they called their son,
the one of indefinite growth,
the one to be lived in, a home,
the one which gives of food
and of water, whose ashes
can be used for salt.

The hour grew more
and more
attenuated:
beaten
metal.

The letter, the name,
the dark, the arbitrary

at five past one.

Sunlight dapples the floor
with milk. Face almost calm.
Boats carry us on voyages
to illness,
to unknown
meetings.

To offer: to receive: to eat:
the symbol
in the exedra: in the self

To offer: to receive: to eat:
the self
the essence
the exemplar

& a contemplation of pigeons
walked self-satisfied in rings
in the serenity of a green pageant

"The birds of Etsu have no love for En, in the north,
Emotion is born out of habit"
So wrote Rihaku   .

& after I had come to doubt
while sitting on the grass
while the air fell, shining sift

Acknowledgments

Most of the poems collected here have appeared in the following books, pamphlets and broadsheets: *Rain* (Sceptre Press, 1974), *The Caryatids* (Enitharmon Press, 1975), *South London Mix* (Gaberbocchus Press, 1975), *All My Life* (Joe di Maggio Press, 1975), *The Story* (Arc Publications, 1976), *Areas* (Platform / Green Horse, 1976), *Moments* (Joe di Maggio Press, 1976), *The Preparation* (with Allen Fisher) (X Press, 1977), *Appearance & Event* (Hawk Press, 1977; paradigm press, 1997), *Primavera* (Burning Deck Press, 1979), *In the Midst* (Stingy Artist Press, 1979), *Background Music* (Tangent Books, 1980), *Unity* (Singing Horse Press, 1981), *Orientation* (Bran's Head Books, 1982), *There and Here* (Bran's Head Books, 1982), *Out of this World* (Spectacular Diseases Press, 1984), *The Claim* (Northern Lights, 1984), *Losing to Compassion* (Origin Press, 1985), *Three Poems* (hardPressed Poetry, 1986), *A Song / The Music* (hardPressed Poetry, 1988), *Messages* (Torque Press, 1989), *Pictures of Mercy* (Stride Publications, 1991), *The Break* (Trombone Press, 1991), *In the Field* (tel-let, 1992), *From: The Break* (with artwork by Cynthia Miller) (Chax Press, 1993), *Children* (tel-let, 1993), *A path a lake the very breath* (with artwork by Andrew Bick) (RMG Publications, 1994), *Stromata* (Burning Deck Press, 1995), *The Book of the Spoonmaker* (Cloud, 1995), *Elegy* (Oasis Books, 1996), *Collected Poems* (University of Salzburg Press, 1997), *Suite* (Longhouse, 1997), *Dark Ground* (Wild Honey Press, 2000), *The Waters of Marah* (Singing Horse Press, 2003; Shearsman Books, 2005), *Spiritual Letters (I-II) and other writings* (Reality Street Editions, 2004), *In the Shop of Nothing* (Harbor Mountain Press, 2007), *Hagoromo* (Kater Murr's Press, 2009), *The Approaching Night* (Kater Murr's Press, 2013), *GLORIA and other early poems* (erbacce-press, 2013) and *A River Flowing Beside* (hawkhaven press, 2014). *Wild Poignancy* was published as the first in The Arts Institute at Bournemouth's *Text + Work* series, to accompany an exhibition of Ian Keever's artworks at the Institute in November 2003.

Some of the poems have also appeared in the following anthologies and compilations: *The Outback Reader*, ed. John Jenkins and Michael Dugan (Outback Press, 1975), *3 Blind Mice*, ed. Kris Hemensley with Walter Billeter and Robert Kenny (Rigmarole of the Hours, 1977), *For John Riley*, [compiled by Tim Longville] (Grosseteste, 1979), *A Century in Two Decades,* ed. Keith and Rosmarie Waldrop (Burning Deck Press, 1982), Various Artists, *Variations*, [ed. Paul Green] (Spectacular Diseases Press, 1985), *The Best of The Ear*, ed. Kris Hemensley (Rigmarole Books, 1985), *The New British Poetry 1968-88*, ed. Gillian Allnutt, Fred D'Aguiar, Ken Edwards and Eric Mottram (Paladin, 1988), *An Enitharmon Anthology for Alan Clodd*, ed. Stephen Stuart-Smith (Enitharmon Press, 1990), *Emotional Geology*, ed. Rupert M. Loydell (Stride Publications, 1993), *At the Heart of Things*, [ed. Rupert M. Loydell] (Stride Publications, 1994), *Summoning the Sea*, ed. Wolfgang Görtschacher and Glyn

Pursglove (University of Salzburg Press, 1996), *A State of Independence*, ed. Tony Frazer (Stride Publications, 1998), *One Score More*, ed. Alison Bundy and Keith and Rosmarie Waldrop (Burning Deck Press, 2001), *So also ist das: So That's What It's Like*, ed. Wolfgang Görtschacher and Ludwig Laher (Haymon Verlag, 2002), *In the Company of Poets*, ed. John Rety (Hearing Eye, 2003) and *Take Five 06*, [ed. John Lucas] (Shoestring Press, 2006).

(I have omitted subtitles throughout, to avoid these lists becoming impossibly long, and also because listing subtitles doesn't really seem necessary in this context. For the sake of completeness, I've included mention of *The Outback Reader* and *Background Music*, despite the fact that the versions of my texts included in these publications were for the most part travesties, pure and simple.)

I have also included a few poems that have appeared in *Etymspheres, Folded Sheets, Oasis, Origin* and *Text*, but have not otherwise been in print. There are even a few poems here that have never appeared in print before at all.

Thanks to the editors and publishers who have supported my writing over the years, as well as to the friends whose loyal support has helped sustain me. I'd especially like to thank Guy Birchard, Laurie Duggan, Giles Goodland and John Phillips for looking over poems in manuscript and commenting on them, as I was working towards a preliminary and then a final selection; and to Tony Frazer for suggesting I should put this book together, and undertaking to publish it.

David Miller
June 2013

Notes

These poems were mostly written between 1972 and 1995, although there are a number of later pieces as well. The reason why there is comparatively little work here from 1995 onwards, is that in late '95 I began work on a writing project entitled *Spiritual Letters*, which has taken up most of my time and energy as a poet.

The arrangement of poems is not chronological, but rather in terms of groupings where there are affinities, correspondences, etc. between poems. (Most of the very earliest poems, however, will be found at the end of the book.)

Only minor revisions have been made to the texts – including the earliest pieces. My use of conventions has been subject to change over time, e.g. using capitalisation or not using it, the lack or relative lack of punctuation in places, ampersands sometimes standing in for the word "and", and so forth. I have tended to leave all this as it is rather than try to be consistent about these things.

I feel that my writings tend to resist genre classifications. I have written a good deal of poetry in prose, and there is some overlap here with experimental fiction, at least in certain pieces. I think that this can be seen quite clearly with a piece like 'The Oak Tree in the Garden', for example. At the same time, I do have a fairly clear sense of certain texts being fiction *rather* than poetry. For this reason I have not included any of the stories from *The Dorothy and Benno Stories*, or *Tesserae* (which was included in *The Waters of Marah*), or the two longer stories in *True Points* ('True Points' and 'An Angel in this Place'). (Admittedly, even with *The Dorothy and Benno Stories* there are a few pieces that have at least some overlap with prose poetry. I'm thinking especially of 'Dream Images of Life', 'Blues' and 'The Serendipity Caper'.)

I have not included anything from *Spiritual Letters*, as this is an ongoing project. I have also excluded the visual poetry, such as the work in *Commentaries*, *Commentaries (II)* and *Black, Grey and White*, because in many ways it seems a separate direction. What else isn't here? 'Cards', which was a collaboration with the US poet John Levy. I would really have had to include John's sections as well as my own, and that didn't seem appropriate in a collection of this sort. I have also excluded certain pieces because I don't feel they are as good as the work in this volume: *Our Bread*, most of *The Preparation*, and most of the work in *The Caryatids* and *All My Life*. There are also a handful of poems from *Unity*, *The Approaching Night* and *A River Flowing Beside* which are not here.

Certain notions and preoccupations surface temporarily in these poems and disappear again – "plenum", for example, which I found useful and important in a few poems in the mid-'70s – or else are seen in a different way. I make no apologies. There are going to be changes over time in the way one engages with things. But I should also say that my basic approach is exploratory and that I have not been seeking to make definitive and dogmatic statements in these poems, but rather something more along the lines of an experimental probing. At least, that's how I would see it now – I'm not sure if I would have put it the same way back in the '70s, say. At the same time, I do have the feeling when reading these poems through again that there is also a certain degree of consistency that has survived the years.

Some of the poems incorporate brief quotations (in italics, or occasionally in quotation marks). Purely for the sake of acknowledgement, no other reason, I would like to mention the sources that come to mind, and also gloss a few references. Some quotations completely escape my memory (for instance, *Colour so fragile...* in 'Stromata'). The poems were not written as academic exercises, so I was not keeping a record of the quotations I was using. For the most part, I can only note the barest details, but in a few cases I can give more precise information. (Why not, after all?)

In 'A path a lake the very breath': *left and right/ gate-posts two slabs of stone* is adapted from Ku K'ai-chih (*How to Paint the Cloud Terrace*), *for the lovely (slender)/ and good girl/ who is my friend* is from *The Book of Odes,* and the phrases *shop of nothing* and *by the way of nothing* are from Molinos' *Spiritual Guide*.

In 'Confrontation': *moss and wild strawberry* (etc.) is from John Ruskin and *the face is exposed menaced* is derived from Emmanuel Levinas.

In 'In the Field': *where were we now* is from Cid Corman, and the lines beginning *and the tribute which he offered* is from a Chinese source (the details of which I've forgotten).

In 'Fire Water': there are some quotations (in quotation marks) from a political pamphlet about the Red Army Faction (aka the Baader-Meinhof Group), but I forget the source.

In 'Thesis': *I go to meet my image* is taken from the Mandaean liturgy for the dead.

In 'The London/Hartgrove Notebook': the phrase *all the apprehensions of his understanding* is derived from Dionysius the Areopagite. "Gold injections" refers to a form of treatment for rheumatoid arthritis. The quotation from Will Petersen was taken from his book *The Return* (privately published, 1975), one of a series of highly singular autobiographical works relating to his experiences in Nōh acting, amongst other things.

In 'Wild Poignancy': *scattering stars* comes from the title of the CD *Scattering Stars Like Dust* by Kayhan Kalhor (Traditional Crossroads, 1998). (The reference is to a line by Rumi, quoted in the liner notes: "We come spinning out of nothingness, scattering stars like dust.")

In 'Stromata': I quote a few lines from my own poem-sequence, 'Appearance & Event' (incorporated in the present volume). Hans-Georg Gadamer's words are taken from *The Relevance of the Beautiful and Other Essays* (tr. Nicholas Walter, ed. Robert Bernasconi, CUP, 1986.) Izutsu: the writer Toshihiko Izutsu.

In 'Moments': *When a line is cut into many parts...* is quoted from D.T. Suzuki.

In 'The Story': *Once more now they are with me, golden ones...* is from Robert Lax's *The Circus of the Sun* (Journeyman Books, 1960).

In 'Moments': the painter Jack Smith is my source for the quotation beginning *the two different worlds....*

In 'Pictures of Mercy': *No time elapses...* is quoted from Shinran, the founder of Shin Buddhism.

In 'Understanding': there are a few phrases from a classic text of Shin Buddhism, *Tannisho*, by Yui-en. See *Tannisho: A Tract Deploring Heresies of Faith*, Higashi Honganji, 1962.

In "solar radiation, wind, rain, gravity..." (in the sequence 'GLORIA'): I have again used a few phrases from the Shin Buddhist text *Tannisho*, by Yui-en.

In 'Areas': *pre-established forms, crystallized by law, are repugnant* is from Peter Kropotkin. Any other quotations are lost to memory.

In 'Portals': *Parinirvana* refers to the Buddha's entrance into Final Enlightenment, involving death at the earthly level. The image of the recumbent Buddha's passage into *parinirvana* is an extremely common feature of Buddhist iconography. Fayum: the reference is to the Fayum portraits, i.e. mummy portraits from Roman Egypt, dating from the 1st to the 4th centuries A.D. (See also 'Aura'.)

In 'Cells': *dark stain* is how Ruskin characterised the photograph.

In 'Threshold': *soma pneumatikon* means "spiritual body".

In 'Bagatelles': the lines beginning *So much have I spoken...* are adapted from a Robert Desnos poem. *...the hecatombs of the concentration camps*: Paul Ricoeur.

In 'Appearance & Event': the epigraphs are from James Agee (from his book *Let Us Now Praise Famous Men*, with Walker Evans, Panther Books, (1941) 1969) and Cecil Taylor (quoted in A.B. Spellman's *Four Lives in the Bebop Business*, Pantheon Books, 1966 – republished as *Four Jazz Lives*.) "Burning the house down..." consists entirely of found material. The inspiration was clearly Charles Madge's prose pieces in his book *The Disappearing Castle* (Faber & Faber, 1937). In *"...for George Alexander"*, the phrase *the motional knowledge of a thing as it is* comes from Gerrard Winstanley. In "There is a confusion of voices...", the words *the stars and wine* and *the song-cry* are from the composer Edgard Varèse. 'Poem for Emmy Hennings' includes some lines from Hugo Ball (trans. Anne Raimes).

In 'The Oak Tree in the Garden': there are a number of Zen *koans* incorporated into this piece, but I don't remember the source(s).

In 'Of the World. Of Power': the quotations beginning *The eyelids become moist...* and *As soon as I pointed my wand...* came from a book on Franz Anton Mesmer, but I don't remember any further details.

In 'Unity': *marvellous beating of wings* is a quotation from René Guyonnet, which Amedee Ayfré used in his discussion of Robert Bresson's film 'Pickpocket' in the essay 'The Universe of Robert Bresson' (translated by Elizabeth Kingsley-Rowe, in *The Films of Robert Bresson*, [ed. Ian Cameron], Studio Vista, 1969).

In 'Three-Way': *not a solid block...* is from a pamphlet by Godfrey Miller; my source is the book *Godfrey Miller*, ed. John Henshaw, Darlinghurst Galleries, 1965.

In 'A Sort of Beguine': *Sometimes she had taken...* is from Liz Thomas (*Dust of Life: Children of the Saigon Streets,* Fount Paperbacks, 1978), *a time that kills* is from Virgil Ierunca (writing on Mircea Eliade), and [the music of] *decay and dismay/ is a sort of beguine* is derived from Steve Lacy's notes to his musical suite 'The Woe'.

In 'Through Fire': *its organisation/ of disparate materials* comes from Johannes Brahms, *what we hear...* is from Fernand Ouellette (writing on Edgard Varèse), *the intellect receives...* is from Wayne Shumaker, and *deep within the soul...* is taken from Simone Weil.

In 'There and Here': *And through the glass window shines the sun* is a line from an anonymous English poem variously titled 'The Maidens Came', 'The Maiden's Song', 'The Lily and the Rose', etc. Peter Warlock and Igor Stravinsky both set the poem to music.

In "The stones at junctions...": the quotation in italics at the end of the poem is from Blind Lemon Jefferson ('See that My Grave is Kept Clean').

In 'Poem (for Paolo Uccello)': *the fields blue...* is taken from Giorgio Vasari, *Lives of the Artists.*

In "The window frames...": 'Lost Life' is the title of a composition by the alto saxophonist Art Pepper.

In "In the blue...": *the wild form of the cloud...* is from John Ruskin's *The Queen of the Air.*

In 'Legend': *...form dissolved into feeling* was adapted from the composer Ferruccio Busoni.

In 'At the Heart of the Thicket': the passage beginning *You collected the bones...* is freely adapted from Eunapius' *The Lives of the Philosophers*, and *I am pursued like a wolf from the sheep...* is an oracle attributed to Maximilla, included in Ronald E. Heine's *The Montanist Oracles and Testimonia*, Mercer University Press, 1989.

In 'Dark Ground': the quotation from Tertullian is derived from 'On the Resurrection of the Flesh' (*The Writings of Tertullian*, Vol. 2, tr. Peter Holmes, T. & T. Clark, 1870).

In 'For Patty Waters': the phrases in italics are derived from the writings of Madame Guyon (Jeanne-Marie Bouvier de la Motte-Guyon).

In 'Devotion': *the one pearl...* is from the Gnostic *Hymn of the Pearl*.

In 'Focus': *Attention is the rarest and purest form...* is from Simone Weil, *the hue...* is from W. H. Hudson, *the double sensation...* is from Roberta Smith and *fiercely polychrome* from Stephen Bann. The last two quotations were both from essays on the artist Brice Marden, from a Whitechapel Art Gallery catalogue entitled *Brice Marden* (1981).

In 'South London Mix': Godfrey Miller and Roy de Maistre are Australian painters, both much admired (Miller especially). *She traps drops of liquid...*: this sentence was excerpted from a description of Liliane Lijn's early sculptures, but I am unsure of the source. 'Briar-Cup': this poem appeared in my first collection, *The Caryatids*. Actually, the sentence *Birds flew over the river* was split into two lines. I'll quote the end of the poem in its entirety:

> Birds flew over
> the river. I recall how
> two days ago
> a girl brought her horse down to the paddock
> to eat and drink

The Celan quotation is from 'I hear that the axe has flowered...' (Michael Hamburger's translation, *Selected Poems*, Penguin, 1972; *Poems of Paul Celan*, Anvil Press Poetry, 1995). *And then I had to look at it...*: Kenneth Martin, quoted in an exhibition catalogue about his fountain sculpture for the Brixton Day College.

In "To offer: to receive: to eat...": *The birds of Etsu have no love for En, in the north...* is taken from the poem 'South-Folk in Cold Country' in Ezra Pound's *Cathay: For the Most Part from the Chinese of Rihaku, from the Notes of the Late Ernest Fenollosa, and the Decipherings of the Professors Mori and Ariga* (1915), later included in *The Translations of Ezra Pound* (Faber & Faber, 1953) – this was almost certainly where I found it. It's not clear to me whether the poem actually is by Rihaku (i.e. Li Bai), though at the time I assumed it was.

Although I don't actually quote from either book, Paul Avrich's *Kronstadt 1921* is there like a ghostly shadow in 'The Story', while "The narrative is broken by…" would have been unthinkable without Alexander Berkman's *Prison Memoirs of an Anarchist*.

A few more general notes might not go amiss.

'The London/Hartgrove Notebook' comes from a collaborative project with the artist Ian McKeever: I would write something in a notebook and send it to Ian, Ian would draw something in response and send it back, I would write something in response, and so on. Ian's abstract drawings do not of course appear here. I've always thought of the text of this collaboration as something that could stand on its own, as well as existing in relation to Ian's artwork.

'Wild Poignancy' was written to accompany an exhibition of Ian McKeever's artworks at The Arts Institute at Bournemouth in November 2003. The publication – a single card in a concertina design, incorporating a reproduction of one of Ian's drawings – was given to those who attended the exhibition and sent to those on the Institute's mailing list. Ian requested that I didn't write a piece of criticism, and that I didn't even refer specifically to his work; rather, he wanted a piece that would be presented *alongside* his art, in any way that I felt appropriate. It was intended from the outset that the text could also stand by itself. I should explain that 'Wild Poignancy' is mostly composed from drafts and notes, from the ongoing project entitled *Spiritual Letters*. A few lines from my published texts have entered this present work verbatim; I thus need to acknowledge *Spiritual Letters (Series 1-5)* (Chax Press, 2011).

'Hagoromo' ('The Feather Robe') is the title of a Nōh play traditionally ascribed to Zeami; my poem of the same name is in a sense a highly condensed "version" of the play.

'The Preparation' was intended as part of a collaboration with Allen Fisher, but in fact what I wrote was not related to any text of Allen's, and the text of Allen's ('Upon Unruled Wrapper') that was published together with 'The Preparation' (in a book with the same title) was only indirectly related to it. I can't say I'm very keen on most of 'The Preparation', though I do still like the excerpt (from Section One) that appears here. However, I was tempted to also include a few fragments from later in the text. It seems more appropriate to include them in these Notes, rather than in the main body of the book:

> the body extends beyond the frame
> impossible
> it burns in the room, a conflagration
> the public square turns black, then silver,

now gold, a
flag
in the wind.

....

sun burning in the lake, you
turn over, my hand on your warm breast. sun
in the lake,
black,
zero.

....

the night moves us from the hollow
into breath: fragrance:
smell & feel of hair, skin.
moved
sun burning in the lake (faster, slower)
zero.

....

the Ferris Wheel turns back, its lights
reflected in the lake.
we return, where we have never been before.

the lake seeps into my side. the body
flows back.

"Apropos of the symbolism..." was based on an essay by René Guénon, 'The Grain of Mustard Seed', but I no longer remember any further details.

'A Song, for Plumage' originally included an additional section, between section 6 and what's now section 7. The original version was included in my earlier *Collected Poems* from the University of Salzburg Press (now Poetry Salzburg) (1997). This section reads:

> how many more photographs
> do I have to look through
> for the *right* one
>
> you are the Maya;
> in spite of your priests

> & your rulers,
> I shall never forget you;
> I love you

Any reader who wishes to can add these lines to the present version to make an alternative version of the poem.

The last two sections of 'Slides' were set to music by Armorel Weston and performed by The Mind Shop on their (our) CD, *Treetop Songs* (Touched Productions, 2008), with Armorel singing the words and John Gibbens playing electric guitar, while I played clarinet. I also read the third to last section of the poem sequence, as a lead-in. The track was also entitled 'Slides'.

'There and Here' is a group of fragments (which were contiguous in the original text) taken from a larger work, *There and Here: a meditation on Gérard de Nerval* (to give the full title). This was a sort of companion piece to my book on Malcolm Lowry (*Malcolm Lowry and the Voyage that Never Ends*). The book is a mixture of informal essay and prose poetry. At the time I included these fragments in *A River Flowing Beside*, I stated: "I have long since realised that I was utterly ill-equipped to write on Nerval, and these excerpts are the only ones I wish to keep. *I am not that man*, indeed." I'm no longer sure of this.

"He collapsed, lay helpless…" is loosely based on the boxing match for the Lightweight Championship of the World between Ad Wolgast and Mexican Joe Rivers in 1912, ending in a double knockout. Bizarrely and very controversially, referee Jack Welch lifted Wolgast from on top of Mexican Joe Rivers and then counted Rivers out, making Wolgast the winner.

'for J.R. – i. m.' was written following the murder of the poet John Riley, who had been a friend of mine.

"the taste of curds…" is one of several pieces of mine that refers to Perpetua, who was an early Christian martyr (and almost certainly a follower of the Montanist "heresy"). 'The Passion (or Martyrdom) of Saints Perpetua and Felicitas' is an extraordinary visionary text as well as a moving account of martyrdom. It has been variously translated, e.g. by Herbert Musurillo in *The Acts of the Christian Martyrs*.

"The blinding moment…" comes from a collaborative project set up by Paul Green, where poets responded to other poets' work "blind", i.e. without knowing who had written the poem they were responding to. The other poets involved were Paul Green, Paul Buck, Allen Fisher, Ric Caddel, Ulli Freer, Peter Philpott, Eric Mottram, Glenda George and Bill Griffiths, and the result was published as *Variations* by Various Artists. My piece was a response to a poem by Peter Philpott. I've always tended to think of it as something that can stand on its own.

With 'South London Mix', the dedication to poet and prose writer Lawrence Fixel was retrospective, in as much as I wrote the piece long before I was put in contact with Larry (in the 1980s) by Edouard Roditi, and indeed before I'd read anything by him. When I included the text in my collection *The Waters of Marah*, it seemed appropriate to add the dedication.

Lightning Source UK Ltd.
Milton Keynes UK
UKOW02f2309240716

279145UK00001B/28/P